47 Creative Homes that Started as Bargain Buildings

Jean and Cle Kinney

A Martin Dale Book

Funk & Wagnalls
New York

Dedicated to all who can see possibilities that others miss.

Library of Congress Cataloging in Publication Data

Kinney, Jean Brown.
    47 creative homes that started as bargain buildings.

    1. Dwellings--Remodeling. I. Kinney, Cle, joint author. II. Title.
TH4816.K56   643'.7   74-12305
ISBN 0-308-10127-8 (cloth)
        0-308-10173-1 (paper)

47 Creative Homes that Started as Bargain Buildings

How This Book Came to Be Written
. . . and Why

As New Yorkers, we lived for years in an apartment where we changed nothing more basic than a light bulb. Then, in 1963, we bought a rundown 50-acre tobacco farm for $18,000 at a court auction in New Milford, Connecticut. As we transformed the buildings and site into a self-supporting compound, we learned much.

With our century-old farmhouse we had an even older barn a stone's throw away. Could that be a rental home for New Yorkers? We could put in glass doors to overlook a lake.

We shored up the barn and remade it as we did over the house. This way, we saved by utilizing one spring, water pump, and septic system for two dwellings! We slid the summer kitchen that stood between the buildings down the hill to become a bathhouse by the lake. We built an annex on the house to project beyond the dining deck and a shed of weathered siding by the barn to enclose the patio.

Each buidling had a feeling of privacy and a long view of the valley, as shown below.

When we bought the farm in the fall, the

barn listed to one side and was filled with rotted hay. By the following Memorial Day, which is exodus time for city people hying off to the country, it was a straight, sweet-smelling house with many rooms. As converted, the barn had two living rooms (one of which was lined with chestnut and had a massive fireplace), two bedrooms, two baths, a kitchen and fieldstone patio. Total cost for conversion plus furnishings bought at auctions, $16,000.

We knew that renters coming for weekends from the city would want privacy. We wanted the same in the main house. To give each dwelling the feeling of being remote, we kept the side of the barn close to the house windowless and otherwise unchanged except for the addition of a shed. Occupants of the barn could not see us, and we could not see them. Still, renters this near to neighbors in the country have advantages.

From the beginning, they have been able to call in the winter and ask someone from the house to go over and turn up the heat, which is electric. Arriving from the city, they can stop right in front of their front door with no walk or driveway to plow through. In the summer, they have no lawn to mow, bordered as they are by a yard, the road, a farmer's field, and the lake.

By the time our first renters moved in, our lake was stocked with trout, which we got from a Federal fish hatchery through the Fish and Game Commission in our state. Occupants of the barn could fish as well as swim in cool, clean water that bubbled up from eight springs, which had been pointed out to us by George Sweeney, director of our Litchfield County Conservation District. "All you have to do to put in a lake is to dig out the peat." He suggested that we buy our lake the way children buy candy. "Ask the bulldozing people what it will cost to dig out half an acre or more. Then, decide what you want." Result for $1400: a pond the size of a football field that seemed in a few seasons to have been in the valley for as far back as anyone could remember.

In the first few years, we went to the country on weekends and returned to New York on Sunday night. Each week we resented going back to the city after our brief time away. We found we were talking more and more about becoming full-time country dwellers. Could we convert more homes from bargain buildings and rent to New Yorkers?

We began to look around for small sound structures that we could move to our property. Soon, we had found and converted two more buildings as rental homes. Now we could live on our "farm" seven days a week.

We employed a contractor to help us do over the house and barn, because we knew no carpenters, stone masons, electricians, or plumbers in Connecticut. One day he bought a big house in Bridgewater and told us that there was a hot-dog stand beside the

A lake the size of a football field for $1400.

Country stand becomes retreat for weekenders.

house that he wanted to get rid of. He told us that we could have the little building free if we took it away. "Maybe you can put it up on one of your hills and start another house," he suggested. We moved the stand, which turned out to be chestnut and a good sound structure. In a matter of months, we turned it into a cabin for vacationers, which is pictured on the opposite page. It has never been without renters since the day we ran our first ad.

We were earning money in the advertising business as we converted this cabin and we paid for its being moved (about $500) and for its conversion (about $9000) as work was done. Thus, when we collected income (which in the beginning was $1000 a year, paid during the summer in three installments), we had cash to invest. We spent the first rent check for a cabin in Roxbury, owned by a home builder who had put it up as a temporary dwelling until his house was finished. We called in answer to his ad in our local paper. "Yours for $300—if you haul it away." The cabin was long, narrow, and easy to move.

We moved this trailer-type structure into a grove of pine trees, preparing to do it over as a lodge. First, we changed the cabin's two tiny bedrooms, bath, and kitchen into two larger bedrooms and a bath. Then, we added an annex containing a small kitchen, dining area, and huge glass-fronted living room. We finished its exterior with log-type siding like that of the cabin we had moved.

Before it was completed, we rented our lodge (left below) from plans to a weekending doctor and his family. When this family left after two years, we had a waiting list of would-be renters. We have realized good income from this lodge as we have from our other conversions, and we have continued to invest. Latest buy: the railroad station below with which we fell in love at first sight as soon as we saw it in nearby Gaylordsville, Connecticut.

When we bought our station from Penn Central, it had a large freight depot braced with hand-pegged beams, a good-sized ticket office, and a waiting room with a potbelly stove. We planned to take this up on one of our hills, but we could not get it up our road. So we bought an acre and a half of land near the old tracks, and this is where we now live. To help pay for this latest conversion, we have made our old farmhouse into a duplex. We now have five rented units on the "farm."

As we have bought, moved, done over, furnished, and rented or lived in one bargain building after another, we have been visited by many imaginative people who want to do the same. Some tell of an old Coast Guard station, barn, or school that they could have bought for nothing, "But now somebody else is doing it over." Others are looking for something unusual but can't find anything. "All the good things are gone." They call us

$300 log cabin is lodge for vacationers.

$3000 railroad station is comfortable home.

lucky. "You can't find buildings like yours where we live."

We doubted that there aren't bargain buildings everywhere, because we had heard when we first considered Connecticut that all barns and other unusual buildings had been snatched up. We found this not to be true. Now we believed we could find things to do over everywhere. We know from scouting that this is a fact.

We decided to show pictures in a book of fine, comfortable homes that have been converted from buildings not put up as homes. We believed that anyone who admired a particular type of home could go out and look for a low-priced building wherever he lived that would give him a start for something similar. We would show homes converted in the East that could be adapted anywhere. As we worked, however, we decided to do more. We would take a trip around the country and show homes that have been converted from odd old buildings in many sections of the United States.

We found an editor whose enthusiasm matched ours and soon made plans with Amtrak to cover the country by train. Going by rail, we could see buildings and sites of every description from our window, arrive downtown in cities where we wanted to stop, and work in comfort en route.

You will find in the chapters that follow that we talked first to friends around New York who have done over buildings in Connecticut, New York State, New Jersey, and Pennsylvania. Then we went around the country, photographing converted warehouses in Savannah, carriage houses in New Orleans, a fort in Tucson, a fire station in San Francisco, and a mining tipple near Denver. We found *dozens*.

We have grouped the buildings according to type, not always in the order that we photographed them. And we have put large, small, elaborate, and simple conversions of a given type in the same chapter. We have included floor plans for many.

Going on Amtrak through towns like Auburn, California, near Sutter's Mill where gold was discovered, we looked for unusual buildings with conversion possibilities like Auburn's towered nineteenth-century firehouse.

Should you find a barn, church, mill, or other building you want to convert, you can look in the chapter in this book that contains what others have done with a similar building. Sometimes you can adapt a floor plan worked out by an owner in another part of the country. Or you can "try on" many homes that began as yours will begin, to see which one fits your family's needs and way of life.

Maybe you will look through the book for a home that appeals to you and find a building that you can turn into something like it. You won't have to search the country over for an unusual building that will give you a start. All you have to do is to take a ride for an hour or two wherever you want to live, as we did in the experiment we made near home. You will end up with more opportunities to buy a bargain building than you can take on in a lifetime.

In this increasingly standardized world, many people resist living in a home that is like every other one. If you are one of these individualists, you will read about others who feel the same way and have done something about it. Soon, you will look at bargain buildings in a new way. Even if you do not buy one immediately, you will find new ideas for your home, wherever you live. That is what you will gain from the pictures and descriptions of the forty-seven homes described here. This is why we wrote this book.

CONTENTS

PART ONE

BARGAIN BUILDINGS WITH POSSIBILITIES EVERYWHERE YOU GO

1.
Where to Find the Place You Want

"Used to be some places around here that could be made into houses," old-timers tell creative people, "but they have been done over."

Romantics who hear that the last bargain building has been converted often settle for a conventional dwelling. Others who are more realistic keep looking because they know that in a rich country where millions of new homes, stores, office buildings, churches, and other buildings have been going up year after year, old buildings have been outgrown and abandoned and some *just have to be for sale.* Time after time, these seekers get a great buy and eventually end up with a home that is comfortable, handsome, and completely different from any other.

These few who find unusual buildings to do over when others say "You can't" have other qualities besides realism. Obviously, they are more tenacious and resourceful than those who give up. But they also have the ability to see *into* a building. Then, even as they look at an abandoned place, whether it is beautifully preserved like the barn opposite, or an ramshackle wreck, they can see a way to redo "as is" or build up or under or out from its skeleton.

A few with the eyes of artists are born with the ability to recognize possibilities at a glance; most have to train themselves to see the frame of a building rather than externals. Both sorts can benefit from seeing how others have redone buildings they have bought at a bargain, which is the purpose of this book, and both should know that there are old buildings *everywhere* that can be made into marvelous homes.

For many years in Falls Village, Connecticut, the great stone barn opposite stood idle at the base of Music Mountain. Then, in the 1960s, Frank Morss bought twenty acres on which were a farmhouse, swimming pool, and this huge barn, built in 1870. He paid $60,000 for his property and got his money back plus a profit before 1970 when he sold off the house and a few acres to one buyer and the swimming pool and more acres to another. He and his wife and daughter moved into the barn which they had begun to convert in 1968.

Determined to subtract nothing from the barn's abundant good looks, Frank Morss poured polyurethane on the roof as insulation rather than disturb the great arched frame inside. As a result, the Morss living room, which has a doorway opening from a circular stairway in its silo entrance, has arched beams of natural wood like the support beams in a Greek stone church. Besides the living room, the barn has a kitchen, dining room, and library and a private suite (on the main floor and in the hayloft above) for each member of the family. And there is space to go.

With its beautiful masonry and dramatic woodwork, the vast home is a one-of-a-kind showplace, yet it cost its owners less than others pay for a home with rooms like antiseptic boxes. Still, thousands drove by on their way to the Berkshire Quartette. And no one but Frank Morss considered making this a place to live in.

After we photographed the barn, we looked near home for empty buildings and found dozens. We are picturing some here with floor plans and feasibility drawings.

Possibilities Unlimited
Wherever You Want to Be!

Within fifteen miles of where we live, we photographed buildings no longer used for the purpose they were built. Some may be sold by the time you read this book; others may be withheld from sale by the owner; all have possibilities. Would you pass them by?

If you are seriously considering finding a place to do over, make this experiment. Look at these buildings seen during an afternoon's ride, and decide how you would convert each one. Then, go on with the book and see what others have done with similar places. Later, go back and look at the buildings again. Would you do them over the same way now?

Second time around, decide which of the buildings is most appealing to you. Look for a building like this in your town (or in another town or vacation spot where you would like to live). Make pictures of this building and of others that are empty or used for storage. How would you convert each one? Are you more interested in one than in the others? Find its owner, and ask how much he would take.

Unnoticed behind trees and buildings on west side of Housatonic River, old tobacco barn (with ventilating door at back) has obvious possibilities when seen from east. Ask owner of such barn to let you go inside.

Shop belonged to stonecutter who collected granite and stones from fields, hauled them to his cottage, and broke them with his sledge and chisel into usable pieces. Stone cottage can be beautiful home.

"For sale" sign on gas station tells you this is available. Wonder how to convert? See later how retired director of Bethlehem Steel converted gas station into good-looking studio in Sarasota, Florida. Consider gas station for studio *or home.*

Old schoolhouse taken over by volunteer fire department is storage place for parade and barbecue equipment. If volunteers build own place or are incorporated with town's department, school may be sold.

Supermarket, which replaced old Colonial on green, has moved to highway. To see how woman who wanted to be close to church and shopping did over village store, see Chapter 6, Part Two. Or make into apartments.

Tiny chapel is owned by association of neighbors which sponsors interdenominational services one Sunday afternoon a month. If the group sells, someone will get charming place beside stream to do over as home.

Separated by busy highway from old house they served as carriage and buggy barns, these weathered relics from bygone age can be converted easily into home and guest house. Stream behind is Bullymuck Brook.

This office for long-gone sawmill has side boards of chestnut, pegged frame, beamed ceiling. Too small for house? Later, in book, you will see beautiful places that started with even smaller cottages in woods.

Once a creamery, cement block and frame building stands beside tracks where passenger trains whizzed by. Can be good country place for buyer who doesn't mind occasional freight train with one car.

2.
How to Look at a Building with a Designer's Eye

As you drive near an old building, look at it with the idea of changing it to a home. Can you see, for instance, how to convert the greenhouse? Once you have seen something similar, you will see possibilities.

Look ahead in the book to the greenhouse in Chapter 1 (Part Two), and you will see what an artist has done with a building somewhat like this. Then you will know how to plan a room where trees and flowers can grow year round.

With an elegant traditional entrance through a portico with columns, you can have an inside living room with sliding doors opening to the living room under glass. In the basic 68-foot structure, you can have a dining room, kitchen, three bedrooms and baths. And in the long shed at the right,

you can put in a double garage and woodworking shop.

If we were considering remodeling this greenhouse, we would make a feasibility drawing, keeping in mind problems that could come up. You will save money if you do the same. Working your thoughts out on paper prevents mistakes.

When we started out to photograph bargains with possibilities, we had no idea that we would find so many. Yet, in a brief time we found the empty lumber barn, water tower, vegetable stand, factory, meat market, barn and silo, gazebo, outdoor fireplace, and boathouse shown in the next few pages. You will find similar ones and more near you. Work out a plan that suits you by adapting one given here.

Sound Investment: Storage Building in Lumberyard Off Paved Road

The two-floor 24 × 44-foot structure has an asphalt-shingled roof in good condition, electricity and several windows, so carpenters could begin remodeling as directed immediately (which is one of the advantages of starting with a weatherproof building like this rather than from scratch). It has no plumbing but is within town limits where it can be serviced by the city sewage system and water supply. So with insulation and heat, either of its two huge unfinished rooms could be made livable almost immediately. A family could live on one floor as carpenters worked above or below. Even the outdoor stairway (rather than indoor stairs) would be an advantage while workmen were finishing a floor at a time and parents and children were making do on the other floor.

The front door in the plan at the right opens from a covered entryway to the stairway which leads to the second floor on which there would be five bedrooms and two baths. (Note master bedroom away from children's rooms and with balcony which once was top platform for outdoor steps.) On first, the side door could open from two-car garage (made from small barn) to family room which flows into kitchen and dining area. Neither door would send traffic into living room, located on the far side of main stairway to the right.

Less than a mile from an elementary school, where children could walk to classes through quiet lanes off to left away from main highway, the home could be ideal for year-round living for parents with young children. On a school bus route, it will be just as satisfactory when children go to upper grades. It is close to Candlewood Lake, where there is fishing, swimming and boating, so it can be a great weekend place.

If you want a roomy, practical home that is both elegant and sturdy, look for this kind of building which can have a 24 × 16-foot living room, large dining room, family room, kitchen, five bedrooms and 2½ baths. And don't worry too much about busy streets close by. Depend on fencing and hedges to insure privacy.

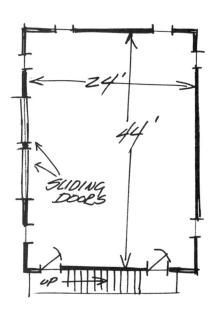

BARN-GARAGE

ROOF

FAMILY

STORAGE

DINING

KIT.

UP

COVERED ENTRY

LIVING

0'   5'   10'

BEDROOM

CL.

CL. BEDROOM

BEDROOM

CL.

DN.

BEDROOM

MASTER BEDROOM

9

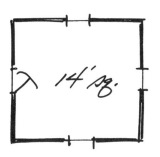

14' sq.

Water Tower on Farm Could Be Moved

On many farms, water from a well was pumped to a tank at the top of the water tower where it was stored to provide barns and outbuildings with water via gravity, as needed. (When the water went down to a given level, pumps started up automatically to refill tank.) On some farms, where water is pumped directly from well to buildings, the old tower may be obsolete. If so, you may be able to buy an acre or two of land with tower for a unique country place. Or you can buy and move tank and tower on a flat-bed truck, which would be easy to do.

This tower, which measures approximately 24 feet to the tank deck, has a strong 14-foot-wide frame supported by a 12 × 12-foot upright timber at each of four corners. All a trucker has to do is lay the tower sideways and transport it to a chosen site which, you hope, will be on high hill where the building can be a dramatic lookout tower. The tank can be brought later and laid on side to serve as wood or tool shed.

With a small 28 × 30-foot addition for living and dining and bedroom area, plus wraparound bath and kitchen with sheltered patio, the ground floor can be attractive living quarters for the owners. Next floor up can be a guest room or study or both, and the top floor with sun deck and breathtaking view can be an unforgettable stay for friends who should be so lucky. Purchase and conversion costs in this case need not be high. Maintenance will be minor, and a home in a vintage tower can be different from any other.

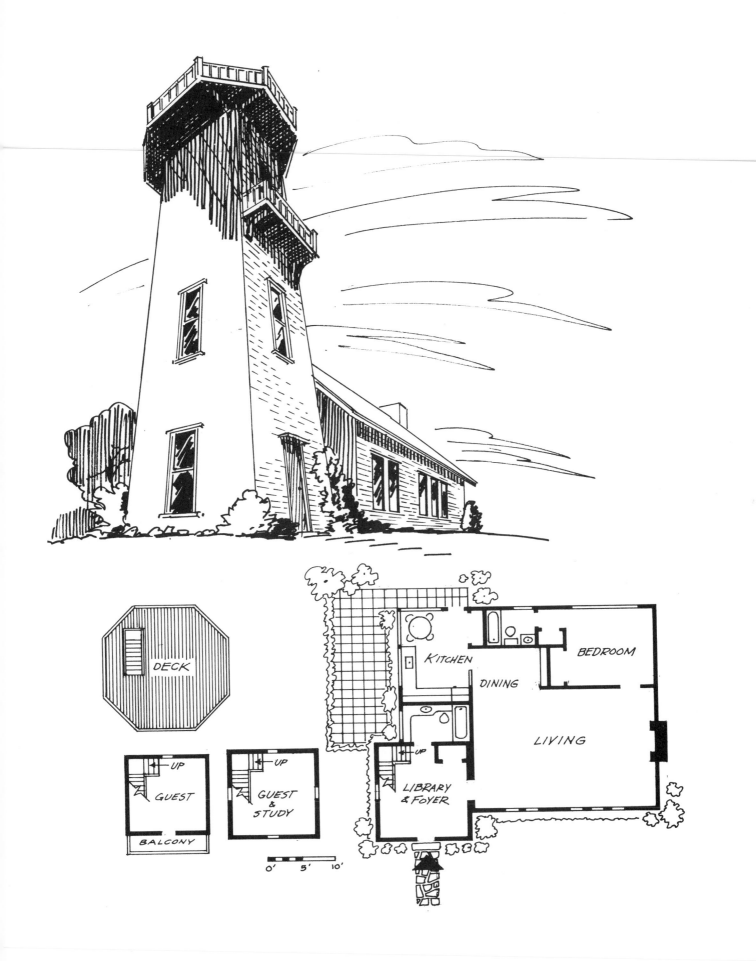

DECK

KITCHEN

BEDROOM

DINING

GUEST

GUEST
&
STUDY

LIVING

BALCONY

LIBRARY
&
FOYER

0'   5'   10'

Start with a Classic Roadside Stand for a Do-It-Yourself Retreat

You want a place to get away to in the country, but you have little money other than your salary. Still, you have an advantage over other buyers in that you enjoy working with your hands and are a fairly good amateur carpenter. Do you want to buy a piece of land and build from the ground up or find a starter building? The advantage in the second approach is that you will have a place to stay as you work, even if all you begin with is a farmer's roadside stand.

Let's say you and your wife or husband have only one baby or no children and have no objection to living simply as you create a home. So look for a roadside stand, which you can buy and move or make into a home on the spot, buying a small parcel of land from the farmer and rights to his well or spring. By pouring a concrete floor and screening the front section, you will have a place to eat (and even sleep, if the stand fronts a country road). And by replacing the wooden floor in the main structure with concrete (which you can pour at the same time you pour for the screened area) and installing a range, refrigerator and sink, you can have a kitchen. For a toilet (if there is no outhouse) you can put a chemical toilet in the shed.

You won't buy just any stand, of course. Look for one with obvious advantages. (This one is across the road from a *golf course.*) First step will be to make your 18 × 22-foot stand (with a 6-foot shed) into a

comfortable bunkhouse. Then before the end of your first summer, buy lumber (precut for quick assembly) for a standard-size 24 × 32-foot shell which you can put up with the help of a local carpenter or competent friend. If you plan to spend weekends in the house year round, you can insulate and install a heating system. Then, a carpenter can get the interior partitioned off for a living room with a fireplace and dining room, two bedrooms and a bath, and you can do interior work during the winter on weekends. Or you can do all of the work yourself, taking all the time you need to finish your home over a period of a year or more.

A stockade fence at one side, driveway beyond the old maple at the other, and dry stone wall at the front finishes off the place. The walk shown here is flagstone.

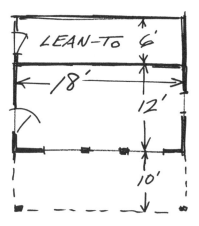

SHED

KITCHEN

PATIO

DINING

LIVING

BEDROOM

BEDROOM

SCREENED PORCH

0'   5'   10'

13

Defunct Rural Factory
Makes Spacious Efficient Home

On a quiet, little-traveled road we came upon this one-time subcontracting plant which assembled electronic components. Away from other commercial buildings, in a rural residential section, the small, well-built factory could be changed easily to a beautiful, workable dwelling. With plumbing, electricity, and heat already in the building, conversion would be simple.

In the floor plan of existing space on this page, you can see two offices at the south end separated by two lavatories (for men and women). To the north is a 30 × 60-foot assembly room and partitioned off section, and a partitioned-off shipping room.

Taking down only one wall (between the two lavatories in the south section), the rooms there can become two bedrooms with a large bathroom between. The existing door in what will be the guest bedroom can lead to its own outdoor patio.

What is now the shipping room at the north end can be the kitchen. Except for the eight feet used for the master bath and small bedroom, as shown in feasibility plan opposite, the large assembly room can become a family room with a fireplace and a living room with its own dining area. Or the space (except in bedroom area) can remain open as one large living and dining room.

Excavated space under the north end of the building, serving now as furnace room, can be used for this and additional storage. The garage addition on the west side will have a flat graveled roof which can serve as a sun deck with steps leading down to the driveway.

Approach to the house will be a flagstone walk which will continue into the house through the existing door, serving the large main room and kitchen to the right. To the left is a permanent plate-glass window which will replace the garage door. Inside this window is a planter which carries the feeling of the outdoors into the house.

Screened by a partly open and paneled fence and plantings, the home, which is close to the road, will give a feeling of privacy.

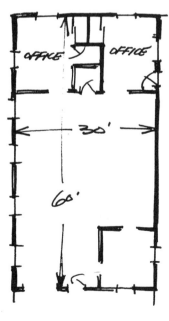

FURNACE
ROOM
UNDER

MASTER
BEDROOM

BEDROOM

DRESSING

LINEN

BEDROOM

FAMILY

LIVING

DINING

PANTRY

KIT.

GARAGE ROOF
DECK

0'   5'   10'

DOWN

ROCK
GARDEN

FENCE

Bankrupt Butcher Shop
Can Be Unique Home on Golf Course

This 10-sided tentlike building, now empty, started out as a filling station and later became a butcher shop that didn't make it. Its unique construction suggests a distinctive conversion, and standing as it does beside a golf course, this home would have as lovely a view as any you can find.

The building, which has no weight-bearing inner walls and only two temporary partitions, is one big room which can be made into a three-bedroom home with two baths, a living room, dining room, kitchen, and laundry. The plan opposite makes maximum use of the odd shape and takes full advantage of the view. Living space is open; traffic flow is easy.

Because of its closeness to a busy highway, the home would need a fence for privacy on its driveway side. Entrance to the foyer is on the north; sliding doors open off a deck beside the golf course on the east. Two bedrooms, the kitchen (which has space for family eating), and the dining area look out (or walk out) to a fenced-in garden. The living room overlooks the beautifully manicured golf course. And the master bedroom is on the entrance side, where a walk from the road goes through the bedroom garden.

Because of its former commercial use, the building has vast parking facilities. A garage can be built now or later next to the garden off the bedrooms.

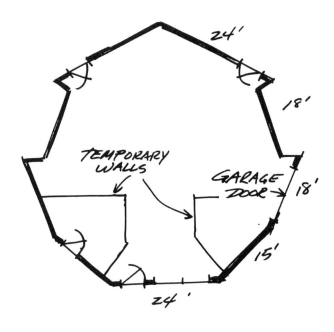

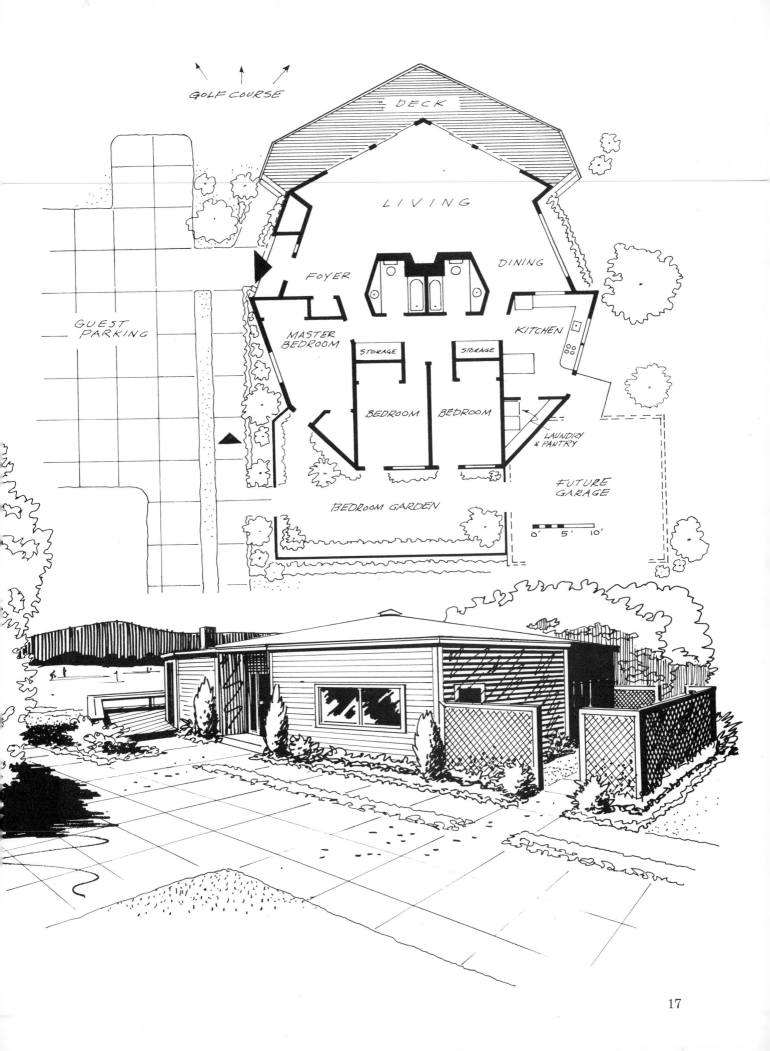

GOLF COURSE

DECK

LIVING

DINING

FOYER

GUEST PARKING

MASTER BEDROOM

KITCHEN

STORAGE

STORAGE

BEDROOM

BEDROOM

LAUNDRY & PANTRY

FUTURE GARAGE

BEDROOM GARDEN

0'   5'   10'

Conventional Barn Makes
Dramatic Unconventional Home

One of today's best buys is a barn on a small farm that is phasing out of business. Here is one we found near us, of sound construction, that could be made into one of the most dramatic homes you will see in this book.

The 64 × 30-foot main floor of the barn can contain a living room with a high cathedral ceiling and balcony, library, powder

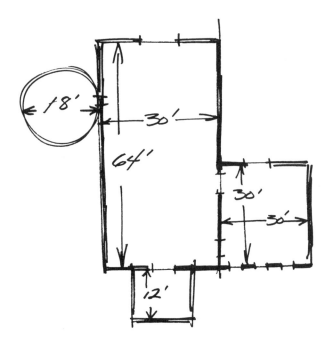

room, dining room, and pantry. The sides of the shed close to the road can be removed, but the roof and corner posts should remain to form a portico. The one-story annex on far side can be the kitchen and dressing room for the pool, which will have an entrance through sliding doors from the family room and living room.

The second floor of the barn (64 × 30 feet) can contain master bedroom, dressing alcove, guest bedroom, two baths, and balcony overlooking the sitting room.

Special delight in this home are rooms (16 feet in diameter with slit windows) in barrel silo that towers over barn. Studio is at top level; a guest room opens off the balcony on second level; game room is off living room on first floor.

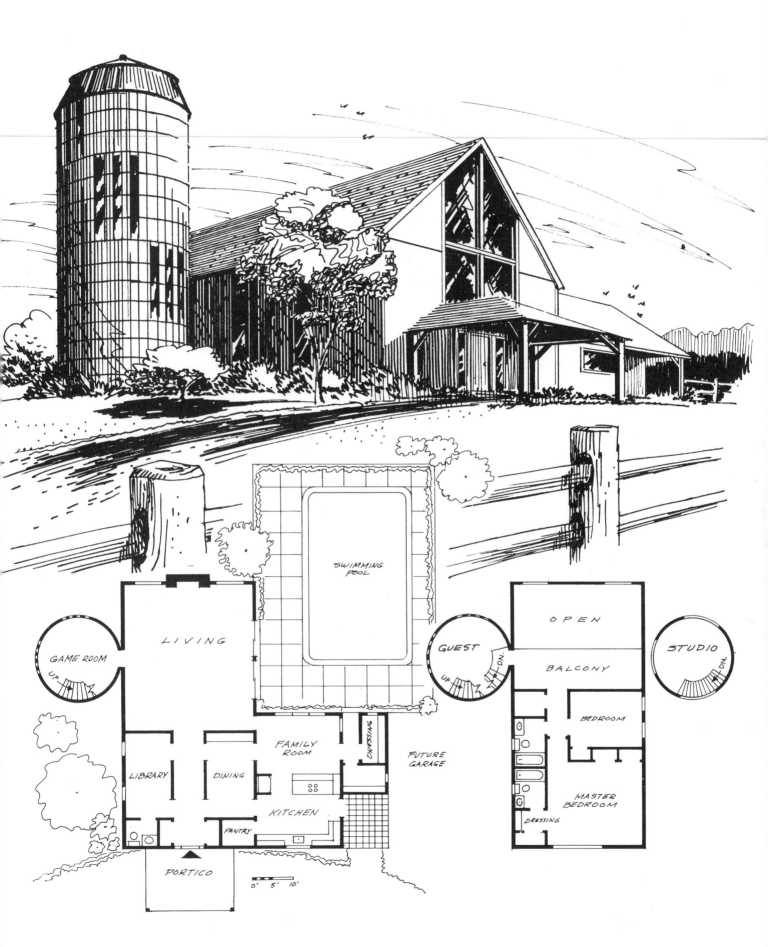

SWIMMING
POOL

GAME ROOM

LIVING

UP

LIBRARY

DINING

FAMILY
ROOM

KITCHEN

PANTRY

DRESSING

FUTURE
GARAGE

PORTICO

0' 5' 10'

GUEST

UP   DN.

OPEN

BALCONY

BEDROOM

DN.

STUDIO

MASTER
BEDROOM

DRESSING

Start with a Lakeside Cabin. . . .

This 20-foot gazebo near water with an addition to contain a living room (with table and chairs, and couches for sleeping in bad weather), small kitchen and bath is all you need for good summertime vacationing. A gazebo this far up from lake, where bugs are not a problem, can be screened or not; the annex can have storage space underneath for boat and gear.

Or Begin with Abandoned Fireplace in Woods

Mammoth stone fireplace (left when the old lodge burned down) would be costly if built *inside* a home, costs little when purchased as derelict. For "hunting lodge," build 22 × 14-foot frame of "half logs" for living room with pullman kitchen, dressing room and bath (with loft above dressing room area for storage and cold-weather sleeping). Put on a screened porch for summertime sleeping and eating.

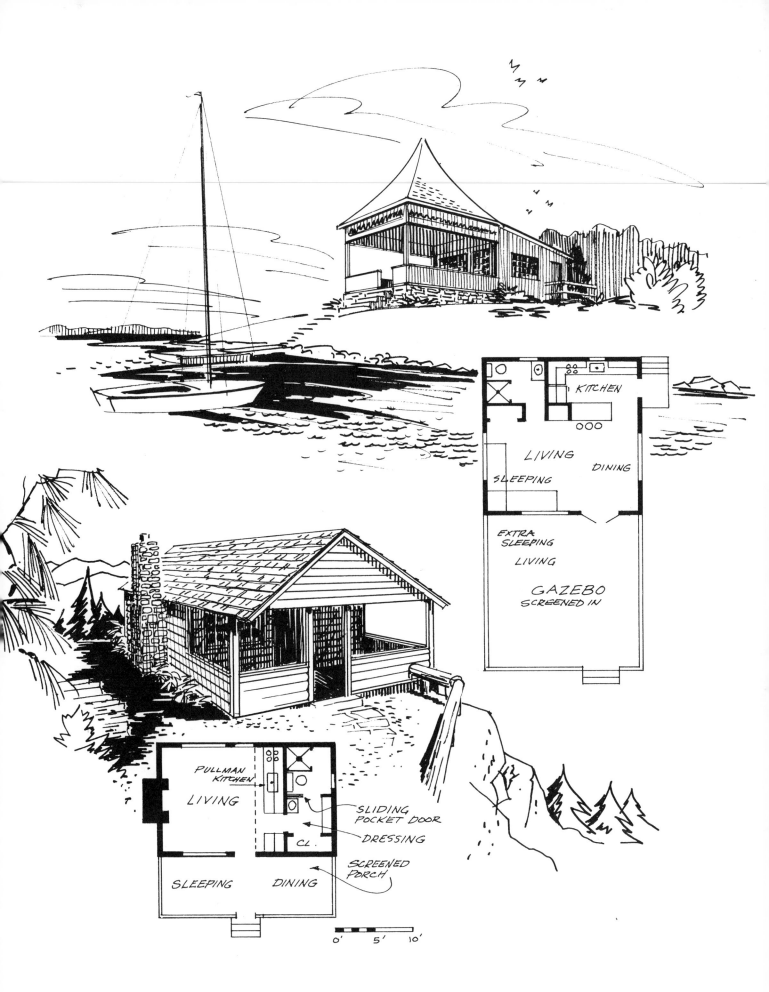

KITCHEN

LIVING

SLEEPING

DINING

EXTRA
SLEEPING

LIVING

GAZEBO
SCREENED IN

PULLMAN
KITCHEN

LIVING

SLIDING
POCKET DOOR

DRESSING

CL.

SCREENED
PORCH

SLEEPING

DINING

0'   5'   10'

21

Relic of an Era
When Boaters Wore White Flannels

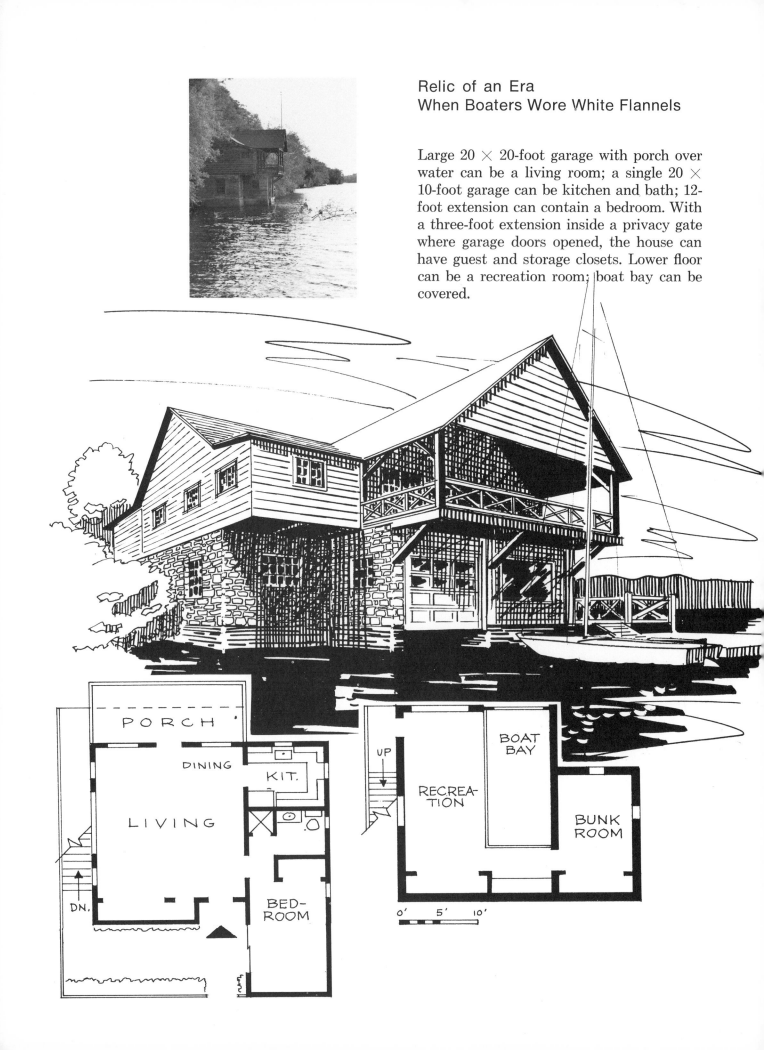

Large 20 × 20-foot garage with porch over water can be a living room; a single 20 × 10-foot garage can be kitchen and bath; 12-foot extension can contain a bedroom. With a three-foot extension inside a privacy gate where garage doors opened, the house can have guest and storage closets. Lower floor can be a recreation room; boat bay can be covered.

PORCH

DINING

KIT.

LIVING

DN.

BED-ROOM

UP

RECREA-TION

BOAT BAY

BUNK ROOM

0'   5'   10'

3.
How to Figure Costs like a Contractor

When you buy, you will commit yourself to spending more for this building and its remodeling than you will spend on most other projects in a lifetime. So figure as a contractor does. And estimate costs like a banker.

Find out from your assessor how the cost of your land relates to the cost of the average home. In a commercial zone where the cost of land may account for 60 percent of the cost of a building, you won't want to convert to a luxury home which will be torn down.

In a residential zone, where it may be 40 percent, changing a small building to a beautiful home makes sense. In sections where land accounts for only 15 or 20 percent of the total cost, converting to a home that stacks up with others is good.

Ask your building inspector or a bank appraiser what a builder spends per square foot to put up an average-size house of 1600 square feet. You don't want to know what he would sell for, just what he spends for construction and landscaping. As you plan your home, aim for one that is right for you and will cost less (or at least no more) than what the local builder spends per square foot. Figure all costs from start to finish, including original cost of the building, plus repairs, additions, heating, plumbing, and wiring. *Don't underestimate.*

If you intend to move a building, figure in your price the cost of moving and of a new foundation. If you have a buyer for the land, once you move, subtract sale price from your purchase price. Add the cost of new site.

Estimate total cost and aim for a construction mortgage rather than a conventional one on the building alone. For this, make a plan.

Make a sketch of how you want your house to look. Mark off squares on paper for the rooms you want to have in your house. (Some are going to appear as you put in partitions; little ones will become spacious when you knock out walls; others you can add.) If you know anything about construction, you can plan before you talk to carpenters how to bring water to a new bathroom through the same pipe that supplies the kitchen, put glass windows between standing timbers, insulate rooms without taking away from the building's character, relate all spaces to each other, take full advantage of view. You may be thinking long-range (new bedroom this year; screened porch next; garage next, etc.), but, even so, put that plan on paper.

If you are about to buy a weekend place where you know no carpenters, plumbers or electricians, work through a general contractor *unless you plan to do the work yourself over a long period of time, and "rough it" as you remodel.* Even then, pay a local contractor a per diem rate for a half day's time to go over your plans for conversion. Find out if there are structural obstacles to doing what you want to do, and get advice on where to put fireplace, shower stall, kitchen sink, sliding doors, and chimney. Do not worry that your adviser may not be creative. You (or your architect or designer) can be the creative one; depend on this contractor to help you save money.

Once you are convinced (through someone who knows what labor and materials are available) that your plan will work, you can buy a building with the idea of remodeling with confidence. Later, if you run into a snag and need help as you remodel, you will have an ally who knows the town.

Check roof, foundation and other areas in the list below as you consider bargain building. If there is much to do, use this as a bargaining point. Add probable cost of repair to final purchase price in your overall figuring.

If building is plumb and true and outside walls have no bulges, do not worry that you will have to repair and improve. A building with character can still be a great buy even with major reconstruction. Go ahead, but be realistic. Make a careful inspection of the following:

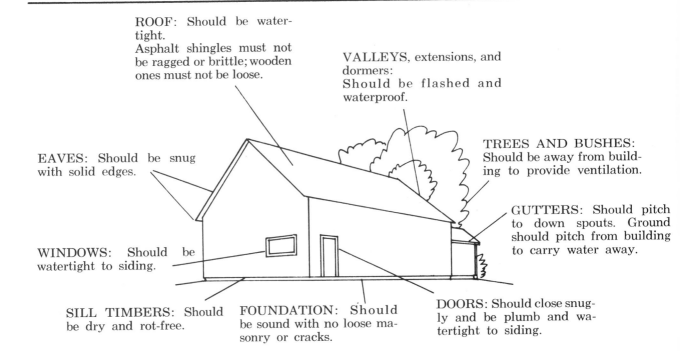

ROOF: Should be watertight.
Asphalt shingles must not be ragged or brittle; wooden ones must not be loose.

VALLEYS, extensions, and dormers:
Should be flashed and waterproof.

EAVES: Should be snug with solid edges.

TREES AND BUSHES: Should be away from building to provide ventilation.

GUTTERS: Should pitch to down spouts. Ground should pitch from building to carry water away.

WINDOWS: Should be watertight to siding.

SILL TIMBERS: Should be dry and rot-free.

FOUNDATION: Should be sound with no loose masonry or cracks.

DOORS: Should close snugly and be plumb and watertight to siding.

Inspect for the following negatives:
- CELLAR FLOOR for sign of flooding.
- CELLAR WALLS and joints for signs of water seepage and cracks in wall.
- FOUNDATION SILLS for dampness, rot or signs of termites.
- FLOOR JOISTS for rot or splits.
- FURNACE (if building has one) for anything that looks dubious (Call heating contractor for this.)
- ATTIC for signs of roof leaks, especially where roof joins walls and chimney joins roof.

- CHIMNEY for loose masonry and signs of scorch on wood that touches.
- RAFTERS for sag, warp or splits.
- CEILING JOISTS and plates for warp, splits or loose joints.
- PLUMBING (if building has plumbing) for outdated cast-iron pipes, which spell trouble. (When you redo kitchen and baths, you can replace old iron pipes which fill with sediment, crack and rust.)

Again, the negatives suggested above are not listed to discourage you from buying. They are here to help you recognize flaws that should be pointed out to a broker or owner when you are talking price. You must be realistic, however, and remember that the flaws you see may account for the building's being offered at a bargain. Balance the flaws against bargain price.

Once you buy, correct defects first. As your beginning, *make a strong box out of your house*. Convert to an elegant home.

PART TWO

47 ELEGANT HOMES
THAT STARTED
AS BARGAIN BUILDINGS

1.
For a Handsome Home,
Begin with a Barn

Whether you intend to live in the country full time or just on weekends, as do camera artist Peter Fink and his wife (who is Monique, the fashion model), consider converting a barn, which is basically beautiful, has plenty of space and can take a minimum of redoing.

Except for the tall windows, the weather-beaten exterior of this one near us in New Milford, which is owned and was photographed by Mr. Fink, whose work is permanently displayed in the world's most prestigious museums, looks from the road much as it has looked for a century. Inside, two huge rooms (a comfortable living room downstairs and a magnificent studio upstairs) have stark white walls and ceilings with exposed chestnut beams.

Converted outbuilding contains a guest apartment, darkroom, and a garage.

Straightforward, spacious Connecticut barn was found for Peter Fink by good friend Sarah Hunter Kelly, who supervised remodeling, furnishing, and decorating.

Glass-walled main dwelling with guesthouse converted from chicken coop occupy less than one acre on bank of unspoiled Aspetuck River in Litchfield County.

Dark chestnut beams in the living room and stained treads on the stairs that lead to the studio look black against white walls. The effect is uncluttered elegance. Nothing is fussed up; yet there is no "big barn of a place" look in either of the huge rooms.

On the downstairs floor of antique bricks is a glorious hooked rug, 18 feet in diameter, given to Mr. Fink by interior decorator Sarah Kelly, whose husband, Thomas Kelly,

a lighting expert, worked out the illuminating effects. The room contains comfortable chairs and sofas, a small antique bed for extra sleeping space, and unusual pieces from Paris where Mr. Fink was art director for the House of Lanvin before moving on to do architectural, fashion, and portrait photography. Throughout the barn, which is electrically heated, there are eye-catching arrangements of leaves and statuary.

"I like to photograph in the country," says Mr. Fink, whose portrait of the Duchess of Windsor was the Duke's favorite. In Connecticut, Mr. Fink photographed Mrs. Van Wyck Brooks, Mrs. Skitch Henderson, playwright Robert Anderson, Dr. Burrill Crohn and Fredric March.

Main living room was storage place for farm wagons; adjoining kitchen and bath were horse stalls. Home has sleeping alcoves, not bedrooms.

Lower living room with its good antiques and airy curtains has quiet, comfortable feeling; studio above (opposite) and immense uncurtained windows bring the outdoors in. Because conversion called for few structural changes, remodeling was surprisingly inexpensive.

Efficient use of space is explained in before-and-after pictures of alcove in hayloft converted to studio. Enclosure, formed by mortise and tenon braces interlocking with vertical and horizontal beams, contains a daytime divan which can be curtained off at night for sleeping. A door adjacent to the bed in the picture at right leads to the bathroom, the only closed space upstairs.

The huge vaulted studio with its wide polished floorboards, glass walls, dark beams, and white ceiling is an ideal place to entertain as well as work. In this case, cutting up the big room to make halls, bedrooms, and baths would be extravagant and pointless.

One Man's Barn
Is Another Man's Castle

Few castles have a baronial dining area like this corridor in a converted cowbarn in Princeton, New Jersey, which once served as a stall for a bull. Nor do many have art treasures like the ones here that include pre-Columbian sculpture from Mexico, Roman art dating back to Hadrian, an Okada pastel from Japan, modern Spanish paintings, contemporary art from Ecuador and Africa, and a Plexiglas sculpture by David Savage of Princeton. But then, few feudal barons had the training of the barn's owner, Patrick J. Kelleher, art historian and long-time head of the Art Museum of Princeton University. And few baronesses are as resourceful as Mrs. Kelleher, who made the mosaic top for the iron-based table with tiles from Venice.

In 1960, the Kellehers offered $16,000 for the barn on one acre in a two-acre zoned area where appeals to convert had been denied.

"Others had asked to turn the barn into apartments or a club," Mr. Kelleher says. "We planned a home, which we felt would be preferred by zoners to an empty barn, which was dangerous when children broke in to play."

Mr. Kelleher's offer was accepted by the owner, who had been herdsman at the original "Drumthwacket" estate, built by millionaire Moses Taylor Pyne. "He could get $16,000 for his acre without the barn, but demolition would cost $12,000. This way he made more."

Zoners permitted conversion after the Kellehers agreed to take away the old garage, close to the curb. (Cost of garage removal: $2,000—so owners figure original cost of barn at $18,000.) With help from William Shellman, Princeton's architectural historian, they made their home.

Twin-towered home was barn for Aberdeen Angus cows. Gravel, new stoop, pots, and Medusa head over doorway (acquired when New York's Marine Midland Bank was demolished) changed barnyard to courtyard. No home in its prestigious neighborhood is more impressive than this barn of the Kellehers'.

Handsome barn had fountain in barnyard for cows and horses, made with beautiful bricks. But buyers thought it was too big for home. Not the Kellehers! They made sensible offer, have unusual home.

To take away prison look, barn's windows were enlarged. Other than removal of curb-side garage and landscaping, this is only change that is obvious outside. Home is now showplace.

What do you do with two floors of a barn when each is the size of a basketball court? With an ally like Professor Shellman, you cover the downstairs floor with cement, imbedding "miles of copper pipe" for radiant heating. You close off the center hay chute for a kitchen to service the banquet hall and informal dining place opening off the garden in the entrance corridor. You flank the kitchen with living room and guest room with bath. You leave original floorboards upstairs and treat space there the same.

Once windows were enlarged, proposed dining area in entrance hall was flooded with sunlight.

Barn door on sewing machine base serves as table for informal dining and desk for Mrs. Kelleher.

Gymnasium-sized upper floor delighted Kellehers, who wanted large bedrooms and space for art.

Upstairs railing protected children and permitted view of downstairs art treasures.

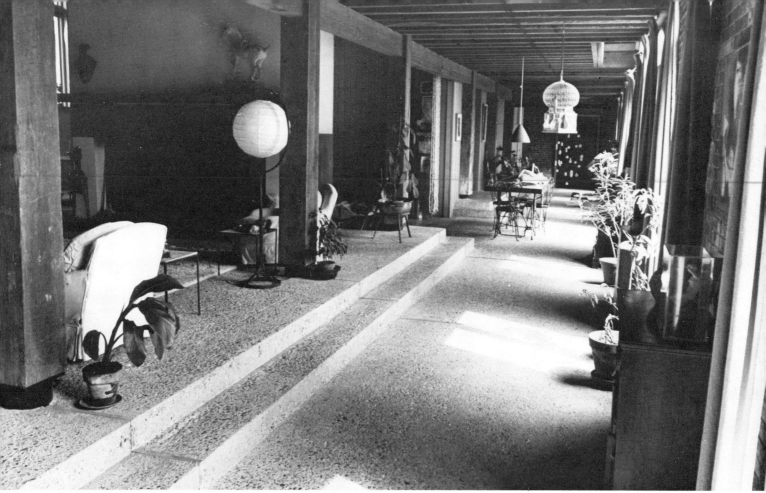

Mammoth fireplace in raised living room suggests hospitality when you enter long hallway, which could be forbidding without this stopping place. Overstuffed chairs are grouped around fire.

Fireplace has cinderblock chimney (plastered over to provide flat white background for African mask and Tang Dynasty horse). Rug is from Greece where owners have small stone house.

From the first, Professor Shellman suggested that his friends "do as owners of big places do in Europe—use just part of your space." Not pictured, but drawn into the architect's plans below, is an impressive approach through one unfurnished wing with a cement floor that leads undercover to the entrance to the garden corridor. Pictured previously are downstairs corridors and rooms which you can check against plans. Opposite are upstairs rooms, two of which were photographed by Martin D'Arcy, of Trenton, when the Kellehers and children moved to barn.

Entertaining is easy for the Kellehers, whose friends, like their art treasures, come to them in their university town from around the world. Not only is there space for 150 or more, but there is table room in two corridors which can be serviced from one kitchen. At the same time, the house with its upstairs and downstairs sitting rooms can provide for simultaneous parties for two age groups with different interests in music and conversation. And both in a setting where art on the walls, floor, and tables rivals that of many museums.

Pleasant room at opposite end from kitchen in downstairs center section serves as library and guest room. Other guest rooms are in tower.

34

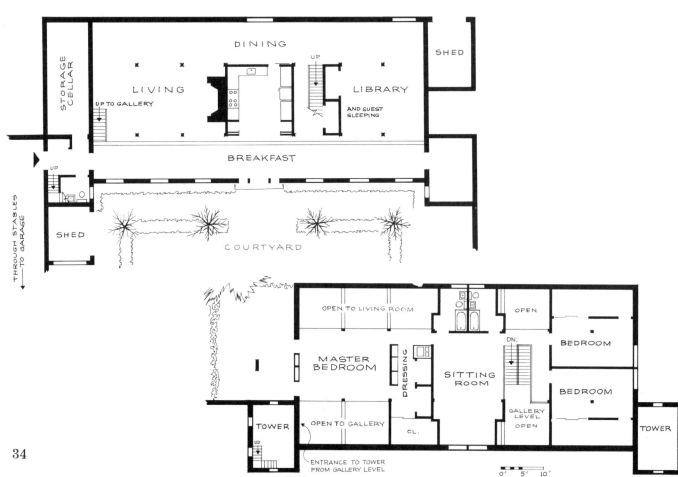

Canopy over bed in room with 15-foot ceiling keeps sleepers from feeling they will float away.

Farmhands unloaded hay wagons where bedroom has arched window with door that opens to upper level of lawn.

Antique bed is Neapolitan, canopy is Mexican, free-standing wall with drawings (left) is steel net purchased from Highway Department. Same net provides additional hanging space for drawings above stairway in upper hall.

When small, Maria Kelleher had room with dollhouse, a mobile, stuffed toys, collections.

Old playroom is now sitting room with TV set, books, telescope, and painting on wall by Maria.

On road that bisected old tobacco farm we bought at a Connecticut auction, we found a ramshackle barn (*top*) which we converted as a rental. To begin with, we shored up the building, then we put clapboard on three sides. Finally, we built a shed to service the barn's renters, which looks like a stable (*opposite*) from the house.

Aim at Squash Hollow:
To Keep Our Barn Looking Like a Barn After Converting It to Rent

"I've burned better barns than that," said our insurance man when he looked at the weathered chestnut building that stood by the road on the rundown farm we had bought at auction at New Milford, Connecticut. "Can you make a house out of that?" A few months later, after we had spent $16,000 on conversion, he came back and wrote up a policy for $30,000.

In converting, we exposed as much of the old wood as possible inside and out without sacrificing comfort. First, we shored up the building and cut doors and windows in three sides. We replaced the chestnut siding, which had many rotted boards, with clapboard, and our barn came to look like a Cape Cod from the road and like a contemporary two-story home from the valley.

We salvaged boards from a blown-down barn on our property and made an extension to serve the barn as a shed which masked the barn's patio. From our house, we could see the barn but not its occupants. Nor could they see us.

In remodeling our barn as a rental home for weekending New Yorkers we did not know, we talked of what "they" would like. This paid off; we have never been without renters.

"They will be coming up from the city on Friday and will want to unload in front of the door," we said. "They will want to look out at miles and miles of mountains and trees after a week in the city." And "they won't want to mow a lawn." So we put a door to open from a parking place; focused the barn's outlook to the valley, not the road; put in a stone patio, not grass. "They will like this," we said, and "they" do.

Upper floor of sagging barn had to be supported with new beams before remodeling could begin.

Back wall below was repaired, insulated, and lined with boards cut from barn for windows.

Once we had assured privacy for the barn by working out a way to separate it from the farmhouse, we planned glass doors for its lake side. Thus, someone entering what looked to be a small one-story house on the road would be greeted by a breathtaking view of trees, water and hills, beautiful year round. We cut two 8-foot openings for sliding doors to open out to a deck on the upper floor; two for doors to glide open for easy entrance to the patio below. We cut windows to look down the valley from the bedroom above and the kitchen below.

We bought wide pine boards we could stain to resemble old floorboards for flooring on the upper level, poured cement for floor below. Later, we would cover the cement slab with squares of linoleum tiling over which a huge handmade rug would be laid.

Back from the road in one of the fields where we had found boards from a blown-down barn, we resurrected enormous chestnut beams which we had cut to serve as support beams for our upstairs floor and ceiling decorations below. From a stone fence which bordered the upper field, we brought enormous stones for a massive fireplace to be flanked on the lower floor by matching stones in the old dry wall. More stones from the fences came down for the floor of the patio.

Permission to burn refuse, piled high, came from fire department which supervised blaze.

When barn was clean, we cut out spaces for huge window to overlook valley below.

We planned an upstairs glass-fronted studio living room to open from the road. To its right, we would have a master bedroom and a single room. To its left we had room for a bath.

We planned the fireplace for the cavelike living room downstairs which would be warm in winter, cool in summer. Back to back with a bath to its left, we would have a good-sized kitchen to service the dining area and patio.

The basic structure of the barn and its nearness to the farmhouse made our planning easy and kept costs way down. By cutting the front door just eight inches up from the ground, we eliminated the need for a step at the upper level. All we did was lay a few steppingstones to the entrance and its threshold one step up. We got by with a minimum of clapboard because we covered only two full sides of the barn (neither of which was two stories high) and only part of the two-story side, most of which was glass. (Because we got a special buy on insulated glass, we could put in four sliding doors for less than the cost of a solid wall.)

We marked off rooms as a child spaces off a hopscotch court once we had the top floor (40 × 24 feet) and lower floor (40 × 22 feet after insulation) cleaned and braced.

By using the chestnut boards we cut from the walls for doors and windows as wall covering in the downstairs living room, we increased the room's good looks and took away the need for wallpaper or maintenance.

We put a pressure pump in the basement of the house to pump water from the spring to the house and on to the bathrooms and kitchen in the barn. We kept pipelines to and in the barn to a minimum by placing the lower bathroom next to the kitchen directly under the upstairs bathroom on the side of the building close to the house and spring. From our fields, we brought stones like the ones in the end wall downstairs for our fireplace and patio, reinforced the old support beams and left them exposed downstairs, took out upright beams and used them upstairs for ceiling beams and trim. With the help of Connecticut Light and Power, we made the barn into a Gold Medallion home (all-electric, converted as specified). They gave us a check for $175 for allowing the barn to be shown to builders after completion.

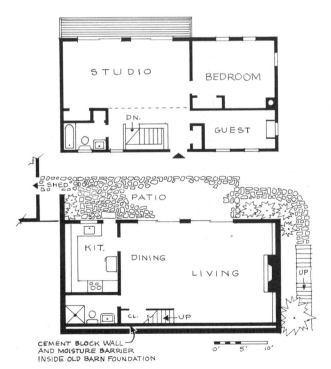

CEMENT BLOCK WALL
AND MOISTURE BARRIER
INSIDE OLD BARN FOUNDATION

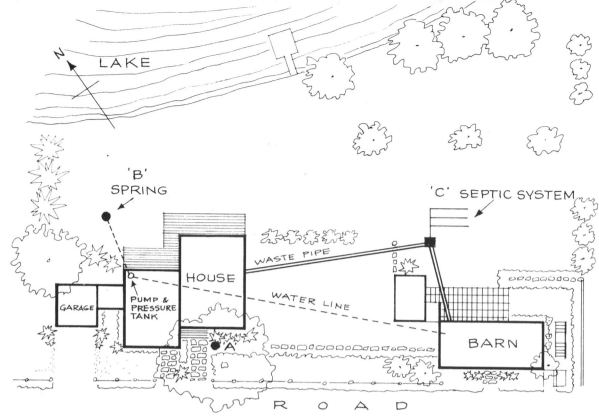

The old dug well (A) in plot plan serviced the farmhouse before we moved in. (Well was close to the house on high side for easy pumping to pantry.)

We tapped spring (B) to supply the house, now two apartments, and barn (with total of six baths, four kitchens, laundry) with water coming through system costing less than $1000 to install. The cost was small when we converted compared to cost for drilling well ($6 a foot and double for casing when drill hit sand).

If we had drilled the well (averaging 150 feet near us) we still would have had to install pressure tank and electric pump we put in basement of main house and plastic pipe connectors to take water on to barn.

Plot plan shows septic tank (C) buried 250 feet from spring, although regulations call for 75 feet only. We wanted to be far from spring-fed lake. Run-off water from eaves and basement drains into a dry well.

To cap spring, we set two round cement well tiles (24-inch diameter, 30 inches high) vertically in muck, covering with cement disc. We back-filled hole with trap rock for reservoir space; then with hay to keep out dirt.

We hired man with back hoe to dig trench 3 feet deep (below frost line) from spring to house to barn. We set one-inch plastic pipe in well tile; hooked it to pump so water could flow to pressure tank and to barn.

Split rail fence from house to barn encloses yard. In spring and summer, lilac bushes mask two-sided effect.

Maple tree, stone wall, and weathered boards (for shed) enclose barn's patio and hide house. Renters have privacy; still, have neighbors.

From the barn's living room and patio, the newly dug lake in valley can be seen through gnarled old apple trees. The water attracts ducks, frogs, muskrats, deer, and other wildlife and provides recreation for barn's occupants, who fish there for trout purchased from government hatchery. They also swim from a floating raft (not shown) in cool unpolluted water that bubbles up from a bed of springs. The pond's bottom is soft and muddy, but the water is clear. Nestled in Squash Hollow valley, the little lake increases the value of our property to far more than an additional $1400 which is what we paid to dig out peat that covered the springs. This is less than what another on our road paid in the same year for a well.

Because we have seen how water can add joy to country living, we have worked with ecologists to preserve our county's wetlands. Now, we are pleased that many of our acres are classified as such. No one, even years from now, will ever fill in the pond.

Upstairs living room has a painting of poultry by co-author Cle Kinney, as a salute to barn.

Walls upstairs are sheetrock, painted white; chestnut panels downstairs are made from siding salvaged when outside of barn was covered with clapboard. Furnishings were handmade or bought at country auctions.

Furnishings were chosen in character with the barn's vintage without being too quaint and corny. For the upstairs we found a rocking chair upholstered in soft brown inlaid velour and a handsome stained-glass carriage lamp at a country auction. We made a coffee table out of a plank of shellacked chestnut and hung a blanket chest on the wall under which we slid a sofa, which we covered in green. We laid a soft gold rug on the floor, matching it to long-wearing gold mesh for draperies bought from the Uniroyal plant at Naugutuck, where designers had thought better of using the fabric for shoes.

Woven rugs were put down in the bedrooms along with bed frames with good springs and comfortable mattresses and sturdy chests found at tag sales and refinished. We used a patchwork spread on the double bed, an afghan to cover the single. We put easy-to-wash-off woven curtains in the small bedroom and bath with windows on the road, tie backs and no shades in bedroom overlooking the lake.

From old equipment we found in the barn, it was obvious that the building was used through the years for tobacco as well as hay storage, for cider-making as well as churning, for cows as well as horses. It also was a storage place for discarded furniture like the old dining room table in the picture below which the owners left behind and we cut down for a coffee table. We found the andirons and the old chair and a sliding rocker at a tag sale and bought the candelabrum from an art studio where it had been photographed for an ad.

With its stone fireplace, huge beams and chestnut board walls, the room already had a richness that needed little enhancement. From a salesman of woven things headed home to Canada, we bought the hand-made rug used as a sample in a New York show. Its colors (brown and gold) meld with the brown covering on the couch (which opens out for extra sleeping space) and draperies made of the gold mesh shoe fabric. Since 1964, when we ran our first ad, the barn has never been without renters, even though the rent, like our taxes, has gone up.

From a Restored Castle in France to a Dairy Barn in Connecticut

Where do you find room near New York City for canopied beds, priceless antique rugs, marble-topped French chests, handsome Italian fabrics, Monte Carlo gaming tables, paintings from Italy, England, and France and a shipload of other lovely things when you return to America after living in a French castle that began as a fourth-century Roman post? In a dairy barn, if you are Sarah Hunter Kelly and Thomas Smith Kelly, decorator and lighting engineer.

Mrs. Kelly's Louis XVI bed, twin to husband's sleeping place across room, is hung with lined Italian silk draperies, which enclose bed. "It's like sleeping in a railroad berth," says owner.

No boxlike rooms for these weekenders in Bridgewater (who live during week in brownstone with greenhouse on top). Their 55-foot second-floor bedroom has a sweep like that of a dance hall in the big-band era. Mrs. Kelly's end contains bed, desk, bookcases, chairs for afternoon tea, large vanity, and chaise. Everything, even Mrs. Kelly's bath, is bathed in light from skylights during day and from lamps and screened ceiling lights at night. Curtainless windows have sheer shades to match white walls.

Like Mr. Fink's barn, decorated by Mrs. Kelly, this one has a vast, clean-swept look.

All of the bathrooms in the Kelly home are large and well lighted. This one has a dressing table as long as most dining room tables, with drawers underneath.

Tom Kelly's elegant upstairs area has snug bed hung with embroidered Italian silk, great window, books, lamps, and comfortable chairs for reading. In enormous open room, Tom has privacy.

Old entrances to loft are now twin windows. Mrs. Kelly's window is seen from husband's suite.

Downstairs windows like upper ones have inside plants and flowers that meld with outdoor green.

Even the dairy cows lived elegantly here. Nine were tethered side by side, each with her own window in what is now the 20 × 35-foot living room. Hay came through openings from above, now skylights; calves came in a calving room, now a bath. Feed was stored in a great bin, now a coat room; milk pails were washed in a rectangular room, now the kitchen. Delivery horses were stabled in what is now the dining room next to the tack room, now a guest room.

For the living-room floor, the Kellys put down cement blocks covered with vinyl tile and topped this with a mustard-colored woven rug. They painted the walls of the room white, hung white shades, and placed four davenports, nine occasional chairs, a glass coffee table, game table and chairs and statues and plants in comfortable groupings. They covered some chairs in fabric containing Audubon birds, hung a painting of a horse's head on the Dutch door, and put ceramic chickens among the plants to let you know you're in the country.

Generous hosts, Sarah and Tom Kelly entertain guests from around the world in their barn on their six-acre Skyline Ridge estate in one of the loveliest sections of Connecticut. Anticipating that they would have many for meals and weekends in the country, they planned their home to insure maximum ease for themselves as well as comfort for their friends. With space that goes on and on, they could put up permanent tables in various parts of the barn to accommodate any number from two for breakfast to fifty-two for a party. And in the barn's various wings, they installed separate apartments for weekend guests who wanted privacy.

Because the barn has many angles, it has outdoor as well as indoor advantages (i.e., each guest apartment can have its own patio). And even Mrs. Kelly's Angora and Siamese cats which she used to show but which now stay around "because the feed is good" have their own "apartments." They stay in whitewashed stalls in what used to be the pigsty. Like all guests of the Kellys, the cats enjoy privacy in comfortable rooms looking out to the hills.

Main dining room has two tables permanently arranged for ten guests but does not seem empty when four sit down for lunch. Plants, art objects, and flowered seat coverings give warmth.

Downstairs guest apartment has its own sitting room, dining area, bedroom, kitchen and bath.

Patio off downstairs apartment gives guests opportunity to enjoy life without bothering others.

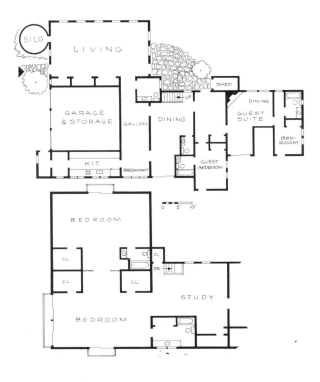

Ruth Henderson, German-born wife of orchestra conductor Skitch Henderson, and her husband bought a Connecticut farm in 1970 that has her converting nonstop. First, a milk-shed-turned-studio for Skitch; then, a hen house for a bathhouse; then, two buildings to rent. Now, she's made an apartment in a barn for Louise King, former actress, with whom she runs "The Silo," a profitable country boutique.

2.
Silos and Windmills:
Monuments to the Land

On an island off the coast of Massachusetts stands a converted silo, painted white and with casement windows, described by former owner, author Gladys Brooks, as "resembling the tower of a French castle, but unfortified, and lacking a moat." In telling of her summers there with her late husband, literary historian and critic Van Wyck Brooks, she has written, "In its graceful, shining stance on a distant knoll, our silo has a look of innocent participation in the landscape, a perpetual monument to beauty becalmed."

Not all who live in silos are as poetic as Mrs. Brooks, but all appreciate their home's three-circular levels, which is the usual way to convert. "This way, the circular rooms are left uncluttered," explains Mrs. Brooks. "We had our dining room and lean-to kitchen on ground level, the living room above, and the bedroom at the top, all three being served by an inner stairway clinging to the silo wall." Writing again of her life with her husband in the silo, she has said, "In our heaven-high bedroom we felt we belonged with the sky rather than the earth, lying at night, an intrinsic part of the stars that enveloped us; at daylight, a part of the awakening universe."

Here, then, is what life can be like in a silo, as remembered by a sophisticated woman, who has lived in great homes and traveled everywhere. Still, have you seen many conversions of silos on land no longer tilled, close to small towns? We know of few takers when a silo is offered "free, if you take it," by the new owner of a farm. Yet silos have great conversion possibilities.

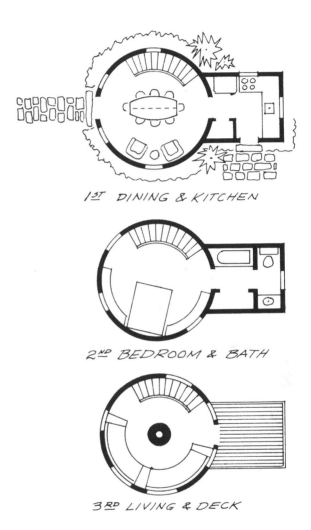

1ST DINING & KITCHEN

2ND BEDROOM & BATH

3RD LIVING & DECK

Usually, a silo is converted to a three-level home, as suggested in the three drawings at the right. But sometimes the silo, which is a storage place for fodder, is connected to the barn. Then, as in the barn conversion on the next page, the silo becomes the foyer, with a stairway to open out on many levels. Or it can be an anteroom in a home or shop, which is how the silo is used on farm owned by the Hendersons.

Started from Scratch in November . . .
Ready for Skiers by Christmas

In the little town of Hancock, Massachusetts, Joe Starobin, a transplanted New York grandfather who left his magazine job to work for his doctorate, lives on 125 acres of woodland near the Brodie Mountain Ski area. To support himself and his wife, he builds unusual houses to rent or sell to skiers and vacationers. One creation is a prefabricated roundhouse or sawed-off silo, which anyone can adapt.

Joe Starobin's silo is 14 feet high and 30 feet wide, the reverse of the traditional silo which is 30 feet high and 14 feet wide. The height allows for a one-and-a-half-story living room plus a balcony; the width gives space for a fireplace, kitchen, bedroom and lounging area.

Unadilla Silo Co., Unadilla, New York, 13849, which provided Joe with lumber, will ship pine or spruce staves for a single- or double-walled silo of any diameter and height, and sufficient steel hoops to go around staves to assure tight vertical joints.

Joe fastened upright staves (tongued, grooved, and beveled) to round slab, encircled with hoops.

Stained spokes spreading out from a center tub under white ceiling produce cathedral effect.

When furnishing hooping, it will allow for doors and windows. For a two-story roundhouse, Unadilla will send an internal wooden nailing ring for floor installation and it can supply a prefabricated conical or gambrel roof. A silo company near you may do the same. Ask. Price will be total cost of parts.

The Starobin house, fully furnished, came in for under $8000. With lumber, this includes plumbing, septic tank, electric and heating installation, and the tricky roof. It went up in a few weeks at Joe's place once he and friends poured concrete and put up staves.

Circular wood staves for a silo are cut two inches thick and need no added insulation when set in a circle, provided the joints are tight. Joe suggests putting a sealer in the tongue and groove joints as the silo goes up. He also recommends a well-insulated roof. He topped his wooden roof with Homasote which he tarred and covered with black salvage roofing.

The fireplace, resting on slab, was appreciated by skiers, who rented and eventually bought Joe's place.

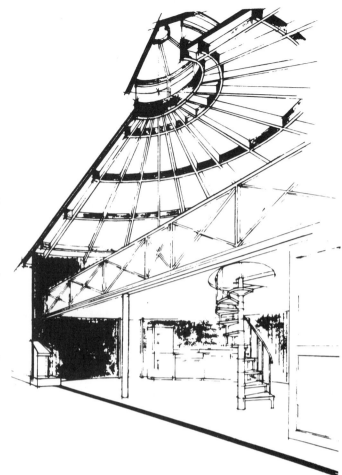

Inexpensive silo-type buildings are comfortable and suggest rural well-being. They are bound to become popular as more people see how attractive they can be whether converted or made from scratch with staves cut to specifications.

Joe Starobin says the do-it-yourself builder of a silo will have his biggest problem when he puts in windows. He must have them custom-made with two-inch frames because conventional ready-made windows are made to fit a four-inch, not a two-inch wall. For his picture window in the living room, Joe worked up a curved frame with two sheets of Thermopane. Instead of trying to build in closets, also a problem when walls are curved, he recommends the use of early American wardrobes or French armoires, which often can be

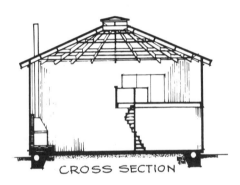

CROSS SECTION

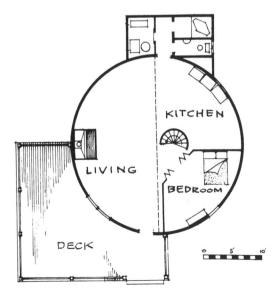

LIVING

DECK

KITCHEN

BEDROOM

0   5'   10'

picked up reasonably at a country auction or tag sale.

The balcony in the Starobin silo rests on circular iron steps, which Joe bought from the local fire department for $20. This stairway is set slightly off center in the main room, so the balcony overhangs only 40 percent of the floor. Under it, kitchen equipment stands against the wall with wiring built into a circular baseboard. The bedroom is next to the kitchen.

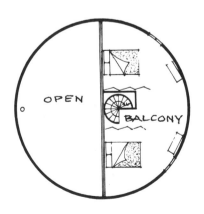

OPEN

BALCONY

Silo has downstairs bedroom with bathroom in walled-off shed abutting silo. This also houses water pump, hot water heater and oil-fired furnace of the counterflow type. Hot air is forced through ducts buried in concrete. Stock louvered doors can be closed for privacy.

Joe, son of a carpenter, was brought up with a hammer, but in planning his roundhouse, he got advice from a contractor friend. "From the beginning," this professional says, "the idea of making a roundhouse with a 1⅞-inch wall to serve as its 'skin' and 'skeleton' seemed more sensible than paying to insulate a barn, which many do. Of course," he adds, "we had to be sure the staves wouldn't separate in March winds, so we put a sealer in the tongue and grooves and really tightened the hoops." Only once, after a dry spell, has Joe noticed a separation of 1/32 of an inch (which did not extend the 14 feet of the staves). He simply caulked the spaces and waited for wet weather.

"We kept cold weather in mind," Joe says, "when we laid the foundation." Because he had no machine to dig a perfect circle, he and his friends hand-dug a trench 30 inches deep and eight inches wide around a 96-foot circumference, sufficient with his tapered grade to get below the frost line. Staking a 14-inch plywood form around the circle eight inches above ground, he poured a concrete slab to make an inverted bowl three feet high at the outside and four inches high in the center. This he reinforced with mesh.

"Plan carefully," Joe says, "and for far less than for most conversions, you can build a great roundhouse." Looking at Joe's house and costs, we agree.

View from bedroom through vane which was covered with canvas when mill operated with sails.

Windmill with a View

On the 135-acre campus of Southampton College, high in the Shinnecock Hills, overlooking Peconic Bay to the north and the Atlantic Ocean to the south, stands a mill that was built in 1712. When eastern Long Island was the "Land of Windmills," the mill stood in Southampton where it was a gathering place for settlers who exchanged news while waiting for corn and grain to be ground. It was also a guide for seamen.

In 1890, the mill was moved to its present site where it became a playhouse for the small daughter of a textile manufacturer. Years later, the estate became a resort, and the mill became a guest house with an addition containing a bath-dressing room and staircase leading to higher rooms in the basic structure. Then the old building, with its huge arms, became sought after by privacy-seekers like Tennessee Williams, who stayed for a summer working on a play. In 1963, the resort was sold to the college where the mill is now a meeting place and guest house.

Like many conversions of silos, the redone mill has a kitchen and dining area on the first floor, a living room on the second, and a bedroom on third. And at the top, it has a romantic plus. Here is a conical cap which, when the mill was in working condition, could turn on a 360-degree axis to keep the big arms (then covered with sailcloth) headed up into the wind. As the top turned, it looked to some like a flouncing skirt and was called a "petticoat." Today, inside of the "petticoat top" is a study.

Anyone who finds an English mill of this type (usually called a "smock mill" by architects because the dome looks like the smock of an English farmer) can have a distinctive home. Because of the cap that rotated, there is good interior space. In mills where the whole building rotated, there was room for nothing much more than the miller and his ladder.

A smock mill is a tall wooden octagonal tower usually covered with shingles. It is constructed with eight huge, upright posts, one in each corner, that rest on wooden sills and rise to the top of the tower. The mill's sides have horizontal framing reinforced with diagonal braces. In its working years, the mill's sturdy construction enabled it to withstand the force of enormous revolving sails, even in a gale, and provided support for a revolving cap, fantail, and four vanes.

The cap (or dome) of a smock mill has a series of beams mortised to its top which radiate to a horizontal framing at the base. The dome is pierced at either end by a wind shaft and winch. On the side opposite to its large sail arms is a small wind wheel or fantail, which helps to turn the sails in the direction of the shifting wind.

In the dome of the Southampton mill there was a windshaft, square-hewn from white oak, with stocks to support the sail-covered arms. This connected with a vertical gear which had face teeth of seasoned hickory to mesh with a trundle wheel. Long ago, this turned the great perpendicular oaken shaft which still extends down through the mill. On the second floor it transferred power to a gudgeon on a millstone which turned against a stationary lower stone to grind grain. Today, the cap, shafts, and millstones are incorporated into the Southampton restoration.

Gathering place for students is second floor in mill where much of the old milling gear adds to building's charm. Faculty meetings also take place here. On sunny days the curtains are pulled back for a long view of the sea and on stormy days there is a fire in the white fireplace framed with dark braces.

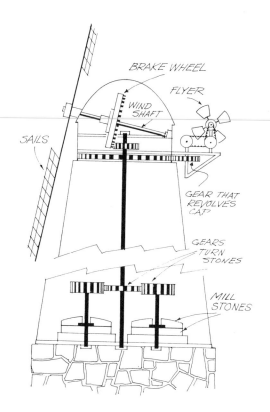

BRAKE WHEEL

FLYER

WIND SHAFT

SAILS

GEAR THAT REVOLVES CAP

GEARS TURN STONES

MILL STONES

Smock mill with rotating cap (diagrammed here) had more storage space than revolving post mill.

Originally, Southampton's mill was built on a high stone foundation excavated to a depth of two feet. Entrance went down steps through doors so that miller could enter one door safely if the mill's huge arms were swinging over the other. (Windmill in full gale could yield 50 horsepower; sail speed was 12 to 16 revolutions per minute; millstones, depending on size, turned an average of 120 revolutions per minute.)

Today, prevailing winds that turned the arms of the mill blow as always from out of the southwest, but neither the arms, now without sails, nor stones respond. (Grindstone frames are flowerbed frames; stones are steps.) Still, old-time reminders are here.

Encircling the huge oaken shaft in the kitchen is a table for coffee drinkers. Steep stairs, once used by the miller to carry grain to hopper room, still go skyward. Old beams and eight-sided walls are visible.

Any changes are unobtrusive. The fireplace, framed by braces, is white like the walls. There are good paintings by regional artists. Large windows dramatize the seascape.

Visiting "Great Scholars" like Margaret Mead follow an anchor-chain handrail to the dome room. On the mill's top is the staff where the college flag announces athletic victories. In the old days, the flag indicated that whalers were home from sea.

WHERE AND HOW TO FIND A SILO OR WINDMILL

In a rural area that is becoming urbanized, you can get a wooden silo for little or for free "if you take it away." (You can probably have your choice of a dozen.) But there's a catch. You may have to buy in a barnyard where silage was needed. Not bad if you can also buy an inexpensive old barn from which you can salvage wood. Buy both buildings with the land underneath and convert your silo, using the salvaged barn siding for your lean-to and trim. Or buy a silo and move it to a desirable site after taking it apart. (A tall silo won't go under telephone and other wires.) Or buy a silo and barn with a good view and convert both as one castle-like dwelling.

Look for a windmill on cleared flatland, a high hill, or in an open area by the sea. (For a colonial one, scout Rhode Island, Cape Cod, and Long Island Sound, where some survive.) Finding one with a spacious interior will not be easy.

Do not try to build a windmill house from scratch, the way Joe Starobin built his silo-type dwelling. Making the eight-sided structure would be expensive, and duplicating the dome and four blades would be pointless if your complicated construction has no purpose other than quaintness. Look for the real thing or forget about windmills. Get a streamlined silo which has a basic honesty and can be a good buy.

In 1950, Alex Ettl, New Jersey cattle breeder, sculptor, and owner of Sculpture House in New York City, converted this outbuilding on a farm purchased from Listerine's Gerard Lambert.

Today, Mr. Ettl and wife, a noted sculptress, live on 200 acres in heart of Princeton in unusual home which began life as a commercial chicken house and later housed calves. Home has gallery.

3.
Don't Push Down That Outbuilding; Think What It Can Be

Drive along Rosedale Road in Princeton, and within city limits where land sells for many thousands of dollars an acre, you will see a long, low home set a half mile back from the road. If not told, you will believe that this was conceived on the drawing board of one of the world's top architects and built from scratch. Not so.

The place belongs to a breeder of Angus cattle who made his home out of a chicken house. More, he did all of the planning and much of the building himself, converting a room at a time with the help of a couple of farmhands, a carpenter, and an electrician "to do the wiring."

Obviously, the designer of this converted outbuilding with its long green carpet of lawn is not the usual stockman. He is Alex Ettl, owner of New York City's Sculpture House where sculpture is cast in all known materials, and monuments are executed in bronze, marble, and plastic.

Mr. Ettl has a designer's eye and knows what materials should be used for what. Outside and inside, he has built with wood, stone, and bricks. Wherever feasible, he has opened up rooms with glass windows in front and back walls.

In 1972, Mr. Ettl, a widower, married a sculptress from the South who had lived for one summer in an apartment in one of the farm's converted barns while she finished a commission. (One assignment: to do ten colossal figures of ballplayers for the Kansas City Chiefs.) Both of the Ettls are collectors, and their home reflects their interests.

Enter the living room (left below) and your eye goes to its rear wall of glass which has pieces of sculpture and huge plants indoors and out. Go in the gallery (right below) and you will see an impressive display which sometimes includes work by the Ettls. The male nude, shown here, is by Mr. Ettl, figures in niches are imports.

Ettl home has patios off gallery and living room. Owner, who admits he's a "compulsive converter," has apartments on farm for workers who mix and pack modeling clay brought for resale from Missouri and Mississippi.

Two workers on farm have $25 per week deducted from their pay for housing in silo. Couple appreciates three-floor home.

Once a Smokehouse

On a New England farm in the Merryall district of New Milford, Connecticut, this guest house belongs to Mrs. Mary Abrons, a New Yorker who weekends in her restored Colonial nearby. Like many outbuildings, this one began life in a hideaway spot away from the main house. Seclusion is an asset.

Encircled with flowers and trees, near a stream for swimming, the once humble house where meat and fish were smoked now has a living room, kitchen, three bedrooms, and two baths. Converted in stages over thirty-five years' time, the tucked-away house is remembered lovingly by children and adults who once stayed over.

Turkey House
Becomes Stay-Over Place at Crohns

Like many New Yorkers, Dr. and Mrs. Burrill Crohn of New York have a country place in Connecticut where they often entertain friends, children, and grandchildren. Far from pushing over the turkey house beside their large home in Litchfield County, they converted it to a stay-over place.

The turkey house had barn-red mineral-fibered siding and a cedar shingle roof, which the Crohns repaired. Their designer outlined a courtyard with a post-rail fence and enlarged windows. He laid marbleized vinyl tile over the concrete floor, left old beams exposed, paneled two walls with barn siding. He suggested a sleeping loft under the peaked roof, a bedroom with twin beds, a bath, closet, kitchen with a snack bar pass-through and the large living room (shown here). Result: good country living for weekending family of four.

The turkey house converted by the Crohns is different from their Fifth Avenue apartment in New York where for many years Dr. Crohn has been a distinguished

member of the staff of Mount Sinai Hospital. Different, too, from their impressive eighteenth-century country house a pathway away, the Crohns' guest house has a personality of its own. Overall, it has a country look, but the country things here are not all-American. The hand-made furnishings come from everywhere. Glance up, and you will recognize lanterns from Mexico; look down, and you will see hand-woven rugs from Poland; sit by the fire and you will be warmed by an "igloo" pottery stove from Strawberry Hill Craft Center in Vermont.

Furniture is comfortable, paintings are by Connecticut artists, needlepoint pillow covers were made by Mrs. Crohn. A cooper's bench from Massachusetts stands by the window; bricks for the hearth are antique; the table for eating is a chestnut slab on sawhorses; benches are hand-hewn.

Outside, in warm weather you can sit on a burnished railroad bench beside a Japanese dogwood tree or pick a bouquet of roses. Or, maybe, you will walk across your own courtyard to Ping Pong Palace, a second converted outbuilding that housed 200 chickens, now a recreation place. As a guest of the Crohns, you will enjoy yourself.

Contemporary pot-bellied stove, which becomes incandescent when filled with burning logs, plus electric heater warm house in winter. Then, guests ski on nearby slopes, come back here at night.

Little house is ideal place to serve refreshments to day or evening guests who play outdoor croquet and indoor bridge, Ping-Pong, pool. Mexican tin lanterns over table give good light.

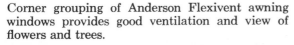

Corner grouping of Anderson Flexivent awning windows provides good ventilation and view of flowers and trees.

Ice House Becomes Office at Iron Mountain Farm

At her 800 acres in South Kent, Connecticut, Annabel Irving, who raises Angus cattle, doesn't waste a shed, fieldstone, or weathered board as she does over one outbuilding after another on her 200-year-old farm.

Recent conversion is pre-refrigeration ice house which had a cooling place for milk and a storage space extending 30 feet below ground for 900 cakes of ice. (In the old days, sawed cakes of ice were dragged from the pond with a hook, sprinkled with sawdust, stacked and carried to the house with tongs.) The milk-cooling room is now a coffee lounge (with refrigerator, table, and chairs) and toilet for workers; the upper section of storage section is a handsome office for Mrs. Irving.

Gate from house leads to front door of converted ice house which has 16 × 14-foot office for Mrs. Irving. Workers go in back door for coffee or toilet.

Wood-paneled room has built-in files, new pine floor, needlepoint rug. Root cellar is below.

Owner salvaged boards from ox shed and stones from swamp when she dug 11-acre lake.

Converted coop has wood trim inside and out, fieldstone fireplace, toilet, service for outdoor dining.

Community Wash House in Amanas

In Iowa, near where we visit each year, families of German background lived communally in seven Amana Society colonies from 1855 to 1932. Women worked in community kitchens, bakeries, shops, gardens, and wash houses like the building above, where they wore wooden shoes and ironed clothes on the second floor after washing on the first. When the colonies, which owned 26,000 acres, began practicing free enterprise, such buildings became homes. This wash house contains two apartments.

The upstairs bachelor apartment of Elmer Graesser, descendant of a founder, has walls of Amana blue, a white ceiling and a platform rocker, grandfather clock, chests, cabinets, and what-nots made locally of walnut and cherry. Rugs, sewn from rags woven into four matched strips, and needlepoint covers for footstools were made by Mr. Graesser's mother, who lives downstairs. A wooden coffee grinder, reed basket, pewter lard-oil lamp and hand-made quilts, lampshades, samplers, and a wooden grave marker with raised letters for a woman who died in 1889 are other antiques.

WHERE TO FIND AN OUTBUILDING THAT'S WORTH DOING OVER

Like silos, outbuildings on farms become available when a rural community attracts new people. (In our town of 20,000, population has doubled in fifteen years, and farms which numbered 371 a decade ago have dwindled to thirty-five.) When farmland is purchased by a developer, the buildings can be purchased for little *if you will take them away*. Ask about outbuildings on farms that are going out of business if you own or can buy nearby land.

Buy a large tract, and you may find a makeshift stable, deer blind, or cabin of sorts that was lived in by loggers, miners, cowboys, moonshiners, or a ranger. Decide why it was put up where you see it. Is there water nearby? Find that spring and save.

Know the history of the land and any building that you buy. Start with a place with a past, and your home will have character. If an outbuilding is definitely no good, at least you can salvage its boards.

Horse's Old Feeding Place
Becomes Stunning Year-Round Home

In 1971, Ray Boultinghouse, New York book designer, and his wife, Craig, who is an editor, bought a 26-acre rectangle of wooded land bordering Route 7, north of Kent, Connecticut. They paid $1200 to bulldoze and gravel a 1200-foot road along their north border to a makeshift cabin that was once a feeding place for a workhorse. There they made a stunning home, as good for weekends in the winter as in summer.

For elegant organic look: circular iron stairway, made to order in Vermont; Mexican tiles with baked-in chicken tracks; Swedish ivy in window.

Carpeted bedroom has white walls with cedar trim, cedar ceiling, large closet and bath over downstairs bath. Airy room opens to deck for breakfasting. Outdoor steps lead up from kitchen.

Dining area under balcony was stall for woodcutter's horse. Magnificent ceiling has sealed double trapdoor where hay came through. Great beams are whole chestnut trees. Stairs lead to bedroom.

Ceiling-high fireplace flanked by ventilator windows goes up 22 feet. Made with stones from fields, it has shelf that was granite grave marker. Simple furnishings make for uncluttered look.

66

Two centuries ago this elegant hideaway home was a manger with a makeshift roof. (The owners discovered that the manger was a feeding and stopover place for a horse driven to the mountain by a woodcutter who harvested timber for a nearby ironworks needing charcoal.) Then thirty years ago, the lean-to was made into a bunkhouse by a fisherman who poured a cement floor, put in a primitive kitchen and a toilet, and bulldozed out two ponds which he stocked with bass and bullheads.

The site was perfect for the privacy-seeking Boultinghouses and made good economic sense. Should the owners decide to sell their front acres on busy Route 7, their home by the ponds far back in the woods can still be a retreat.

They have invested $55,000 to transform the cabin, which had one room and a loft, into a showplace with a two-car garage. Downstairs, they have a living room, dining area, kitchen, glassed-in porch, bath and closets; upstairs, a bedroom, closet, bath and deck. They have extended the cement floor to measure 19 × 35 feet which they covered with Mexican tiles, and have made other ambitious changes. So, why start with an old building?

"The site overlooking the ponds was cleared," says Ray, "and we had the retaining wall, beams, and history, which we appreciate."

Owners had right to spring water from neighboring property but drilled an Artesian well (180 feet deep, 15 gallons a minute) for a cost of $2000 for an abundant

Below railed deck on entrance side of house is spacious room with sliding glass walls that converts to screened sleeping porch for guests. Windows have plants, not curtains; siding is redwood.

water supply. Thinking long-term, they resisted skimping anywhere. They put in windows (some stock, some made to measure) three, six, and ten feet for ventilation and lighting. Their mason laid stone on stone for a giant fireplace; carpenters bleached redwood siding with special oils; Vermont craftsmen made the circular iron staircase with Nova Scotia oak treads for $450 f.o.b.

Biggest problem: laying do-it-yourself Mexican tiles. Making decision not to tint tiles, as some do, they went to work, but soon turned the job over to professionals who laid the squares in two weeks. (Base cement floor had to be cured before tiles went down; spaces between laid tiles had to be grouted; tiles had to be washed with acid, treated with boiled linseed oil, rinsed with turpentine.) After the tiles had dried for two weeks, the Boultinghouses, on hands and knees, polished them with butcher's wax. Now each tile is a picture.

"Not easy but satisfying," said Mrs. Boultinghouse at the end of the first year, and her husband, whose investment totaled $81,000, added, "Not cheap, but a good buy." Now these remodelers want to do more.

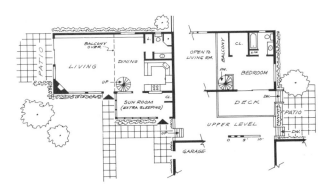

"I Like to See the Ocean"

That's what Gary Merrill said in '71 when he bought lighthouse for about $25,000 at Cape Elizabeth, Maine. Owner had bought tower with 6000 square feet of land as government surplus.

Actor's light, which had appeared on Maine's sesquicentennial postage stamp, attracted so much publicity, retreat for Merrill was impossible. In year, he listed light for $60,000.

4.
How to Buy Waterfront Property Without Spending a Fortune

One of the best buys you can get is a lighthouse, *especially when you buy direct from the government.* Many types—cylindrical structures with stone or cast-iron towers, frame dwellings with a light above, and compounds with homes separate from the tower—have been sold to private parties by the General Services Administration when such lights were no longer needed by the Coast Guard. Some are Table Bluff Light, 15 miles southwest of Eureka, California; Bolivar Light, 15 miles southwest of Galveston, Texas; Great Captain Island Light in Captain Harbor, Greenwich, Connecticut; New London Harbor Light on the west side of the entrance to New London Harbor, Connecticut; Big Bay Light on Lake Superior. All are naturally dramatic, and all were bargains when purchased through a sealed bid or at auction.

Because a Coast Guard light is a home for one or more employees, it often can be lived in "as is" by a purchaser, who pays far less than the government spent for the property. The cast-iron tower on Merrill's lighthouse cost Uncle Sam $15,000. And Bolivar Point Lighthouse, purchased by a rancher in the '40s for a reputed $5500, had an assessed value in the '30s of $97,500 ($2500 for two acres of land and $95,000 for "improvements"). This Texas landmark has two residences flanking the original brick tower, which has cast-iron sides bolted to the ground. (During the great storm of 1900, one hundred evacuees found refuge there.) The view from top of 157 corkscrew steps is spectacular as is the outlook from Big Bay Lighthouse below.

Doctor's lighthouse at Big Bay, Michigan, has breathtaking view, was breathtaking bargain at $4000.

GLAMOROUS INSIDE. That's the consensus of visitors to Michigan's Big Bay Lighthouse, with an interior refurbished from top to bottom by Dr. John Pick, internationally known plastic surgeon from Chicago, who bought with sealed bid.

When purchased in 1961, the building had two identical units, each of which had a dozen rooms 11.5 × 14.2 feet in size. Built in 1867 for a Scottish lighthouse keeper and his helper and their families, the two dwellings, which had matching front and back entrances, were joined upstairs and down through community family rooms in a central optics tower which rose 174 feet above the level of Lake Superior. Upstairs, the family room doubled as a chapel; downstairs, a similar room served once a week as a schoolroom for eleven children belonging to the keeper, his helper, and another worker who lived on Marquette County's Big Bay Point. Otherwise, the room was an office for the Coast Guard chief. Now, the two units are one 18-room dwelling. The center section still towers.

A world traveler and scholar, Dr. Pick respects the design and history of his lighthouse home. His new fireplace, like the old building, is brick, as are the dining-room walls. Old hardwood floors, from which carpenters scraped five coats of paint, look new. At top center is a sunny room with round walls and floors.

In the tower, Dr. Pick points out two slits in each floor which are joined by a winding metal stairway. "Twin chains fell through these slits so that the keeper could manipulate the beacon from below." Calling attention to a long chimney on the fog house next to the lighthouse, he says, "In a dense fog when northerly winds prevented audio contact with ships, the keeper shot balls of flame out of the chimney." He points to a 75-foot pier below the cliffs on which the 86-foot-high lighthouse was built. "Construction supplies were delivered after President Lincoln had commissioned an Englishman to design the place."

70

GLORIOUS OUTSIDE when seen from land or sea.

Designed like an old Scottish castle, the novel vacation house of Dr. Pick now has eighteen rooms which include seven bedrooms, many baths, large-scale living and dining areas, indoor and outdoor breakfast places, two optics rooms, and a glassed-in cupola. In every room are priceless antiques. One chest was presented to General Grant by President Lincoln; a steering wheel from the *Normandie* came to Dr. Pick from a French ambassador; ivory wall hangings were once in the Vatican; a sculptured god of water came from Honduras.

With all the remodeling, the exterior hasn't changed much in a century. Built on a stone-and-concrete foundation, this lighthouse has red brick walls, a metal roof and a brass cupola, and at just $4000 has to be one of the best bargains by almost anyone in twenty-five years.

An admirer of lighthouses since childhood, Dr. Pick knew he wanted the uninhabited tower at Big Bay, Michigan, the minute he read the sale notice in the lobby of Chicago's main Post Office. With forty-eight other lighthouse buffs, he submitted an offer to buy and was notified that his bid of $4000 was $400 higher than any other. So, in October, 1961, he found himself the owner of a lighthouse, fog house, oil building, and two outhouses on 38½ acres of land (with

4000 feet of shoreline) on the south shore of Lake Superior.

Dr. Pick says he arrived at his lighthouse and was told by a local contractor, "You're a damn fool." A few years later, he heard from this same man: "You were smarter than any of us." Smarter, luckier, whatever, Dr. Pick has spent less for his lakeside retreat than others spend for a split-level ranch. He got the end-all buy!

HOW TO BUY A BUILDING THROUGH GSA

GSA sells lighthouses, forts, hospitals, fire-spotting towers, boats, barges, schools, chapels, warehouses and other buildings for Federal agencies that no longer need such properties. To find what is being sold when, write to General Services Administration, Washington, D.C. 20405, for addresses of its ten regional offices in Boston, New York City, Washington, D.C., Atlanta, Chicago, Kansas City, Fort Worth, Denver, San Francisco, and Auburn, Washington.

Ask one or all GSA offices to put you on mailing list for sales of buildings in given price range. When a building interests you, ask for an *Invitation to Bid* form, which explains terms. (Usually, you must send 10 percent in cash with your offer. If high with sealed bid or at auction, you can pay 25 percent in cash and the remainder in eight or ten years at reasonable interest.) All property is sold "as is, where is," so inspect if possible.

Artist owner, who selected colors for Savannah project, chose greenish black Swamp Root paint for shutters, Geechee Teal for trim. She and husband live on top floors opening to Bay Street.

The Osteens selected wheel of Georgia pine for interior focal point. Recorded in Library of Congress, it was hand-hewn by Geechee slaves, served as upright pulley wheel for cotton lift.

Georgia Ballast Building Takes on New Life

In 1972, Dr. Clark Osteen and his wife, Ann, long-time president of Savannah's Art Association, bought a cotton warehouse in Savannah's 2½-square-mile historic center designated as a landmark by the National Park Service. Authorities say the building, which has four floors plus a basement and attic, is the oldest in Georgia constructed of rubble, cobblestones, Dutch and Roman bricks, coral, lava, and other ballast stones used to stabilize ships that came to America for cotton. The Osteens preserved its exterior but did over the interior to fit their life.

In this century, the building, known to have been standing in 1817, has served as a chandlery which supplied repair materials, navigational aids, and other equipment to ships leaving for sea from the Savannah River, which runs a few feet from its north side. Its thick walls were repaired after an earthquake in 1881 but are structurally sound, double doors on each floor have their original hardware, tin roof is sound. Owners' pride: 11-foot lifting wheel for elevator cable hand-made by slaves.

Property purchased by Osteens for $33,000 stands at Bull and Bay where General Oglethorpe, Savannah's founder, arrived from England in 1733. Lower floors are rented as shops.

Architect Juan C. Bertotto suspended wheel from tie beams, planned skylight view of river.

Looking down from balcony, note brick-lined entrance at right, curved wall that encloses kitchen.

Colorful factors' walk where brokers inspected cotton has underground latrines paved with oyster shells. When Osteens bought buildings, bums were living under entrance way. Today, home is historical showplace.

Ballast stone wall and heart-pine stairway enrich living room which adjoins master bedroom and bath. Looking up, visitor can see hand-hewn wheel and Georgia's sunny sky.

California Fisherman's Shack Becomes Palace of Light

Until around 1937, Sausalito, across the Bay from San Francisco, was a sleepy fisherman's village, and this sunlit home was the old Johannesen place. Then came Golden Gate Bridge, bringing vacationers and commuters. Overnight, Sausalito became a boom town, and its old Scandinavian section became legendary. (Jack London supposedly "dried out" in a house near here.) Some of the fishermen's houses lost their charm as they were sold and remade but others like this one, owned by Betty Rogers, benefited from changes made by successive owners.

In 1906, the fisherman here had a marine track from the Bay to his house so that his boat could be hauled in for repair. Now this boat shed is a rental apartment with one of the few waterfront lawns on San Francisco Bay. Above is Mrs. Rogers' two-floor home.

Like the prow of a ship, the double-story bay window, which fronts Mrs. Rogers' living room and upstairs bedroom (opposite), looks out at sun-glistened water, alive with gulls, pelicans, loons and sloops. In the spring, which is when we were there, sea breezes bring the fragrance of California lilacs, Texas privet, and blossoming lemon trees. Daffodils splash color outside and in.

This beach house and the one next door, also owned by Mrs. Rogers, are assessed at $137,000; the done-over shack at $90,000. Several architects, including internationally known Dorothy Alexander (who planned the bay window and spiral staircase when the house was rebuilt in 1963), deserve credit.

Entry to the house, shingled with No. 1 Cedar shake, is from the street through a narrow passageway along a brick walk to a privet-bordered garden and outdoor dining area on a wooden patio.

The door opens to an indoor dining area where the eye travels on through the bay window to a long-range view of Alcatraz.

Approach through privet garden leads to door that opens between closed-off kitchen and dining area. Wooden patio extends home's living space.

Featured for its "ultramodern architecture" in Chamber of Commerce brochure, old building, now remodeled, has view of Angel Island and Alcatraz.

Eye is led past closed-off garden kitchen and
open dining room to sunlit view of bay.

Furnishings are eclectic, but light walls and glass table give Scandinavian feeling.

Mrs. Rogers' home is furnished with classics from everywhere. One French secretary from a Palace of Napoleon III, used now as bar, belonged to the owner's great-grandparents; a fifteenth-century prayer desk is from Spain; rare lithographs are English; hand-crafted sterling silver was presented to Mrs. Rogers' grandparents in recognition of long-time service to the city of Pittsburgh. Airy open rooms are wonderfully light.

Beautiful woods enrich downstairs rooms. Kitchen cabinets are matched walnut as are shelves by the pedestal fireplace and its mantel. Except for the kitchen, all downstairs walls are paneled in California redwood, brushed with white. Beams and valances are stained brown-black against white ceilings.

Fireplace tiles are unglazed, slipcovers are linen, glass tables, designed by Mrs. Rogers, do nothing to interrupt the sweep of green avocado carpeting in the living and dining room and on the treads of the steps on the iron stairway. Low chairs, tall plants, and the two floor windows also uplift.

Walls of the stairwell are white plaster like the ceilings, and carpeting upstairs is white. Walls of the bedroom are papered as are walls and shades in the kitchen. Beautifully groomed plants, seascapes by California artists, and a Scandinavian mobile bring in the feeling of the outdoors. Breezes from the Bay do the air-conditioning.

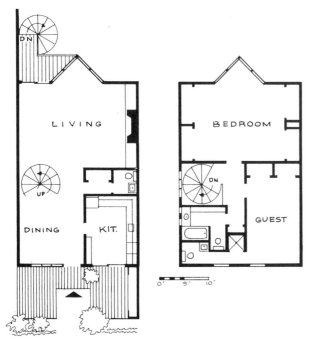

Like the town of Sausalito, originally called Saucelito, which means "little willow" in Spanish, Mrs. Rogers' home is a fairytale place, outside and in. Walk between ivy-covered walls from Bridgeway Street and you come to a fifty-year-old Gravenstein apple tree that still bears fruit, and sweet-smelling Texas privet, cut like topiaries and potted in immense clay pots topped with flat gray stones from a Japanese nursery. Lemon trees border the wooden patio with its wrought-iron chairs and a glass-topped table.

Inside, everything is blue and white on green. Exotic seashells catch your eye in a Steuben bowl; a ship model and original designer's profiles for sailboats are on the wall; glass birds stand on glass tables; the owner's sailboat and dinghy are anchored in the green-blue water outside.

Plaited canvas shades in the living room and bedroom can be pulled when too much sun pours in; shades in the kitchen are mostly for decoration. Breakfast on the patio in the garden is a delight in the morning; dinner inside, looking out to lights on the water, is an unforgettable experience at night. The best of indoor living and outdoor living—this house has it all!

According to Betty Rogers, who teaches in a West Coast college, sailors from nineteenth-century whaling ships used to pull in at the cove out front to peddle their "take" to residents without bothering to register their cargo, which was required in major ports, thus avoiding taxation. Such sailors might well recognize Mrs. Rogers' unusual furnishings which have been brought across the water from everywhere. Rare but unobtrusive, they add richness to the house as do the custom-made sofa and chairs, covered in hand-appliquéd linen.

At night, the lights of Berkeley are visible; by day, sunshine and soft breezes come through windows. Flowers and plants are everywhere. The old Johannesen place is alive.

In the upstairs bath, two slanted windows and a central mirror of the same size have been inserted between rafters of the gambrel roof; on the stairwell, three panels of pebbled glass are also between rafters. No curtains keep out sunshine and sky.

LOOK BESIDE WATER ANYWHERE FOR UNUSUAL BUILDINGS

Best way to get a waterfront bargain is to buy an old building that others pass up. A good way to find one is to look for deserted lighthouse, boathouse, cottage, pumphouse, or fisherman's shacks by a river, lake or beach where you could enjoy life. Don't neglect boats. (One $2 million concrete tanker was sold for $100.) Often sold as surplus real property, they can be bargains and involve no expense for land.

When you ask about sales at GSA regional offices, write also to the departments of Defense, Agriculture, and Interior. These departments (rather than GSA) dispose of land and improvements when the fair market value is less than $1000. At such sales, boats and barges (especially those used by DOD) and small buildings go on block.

For quick news of government sales, you can subscribe to *Commerce Business Daily* through Superintendent of Documents, Washington, D.C. 20402. Annual cost: $25.

Historic Bolivar Light and two caretaker cottages stood empty for fourteen years until bought in 1947 as government surplus by E. V. Boyt, of Texas. Later, Mr. Boyt rented light to film company for *My Sweet Charlie*.

Watercolor by Cyril A. Lewis pictures lovely old landmark on Long Island Sound owned since 1938 by the village of Old Field. New oil burner and kitchen are only changes in 1868 light, now policeman's home.

Burned-out boathouse on Lake Waramaug, Connecticut's largest natural lake, stands on concrete bulkhead on natural point. Structure is sound, charred boards can be scraped, building can be deodorized with chemicals.

Houseboat in San Francisco Bay shows what can be done with a barge, which can be bargain when bought from water transport contractor or as Department of Transportation discard. No land to buy here.

CONVERTED BY CLAY SHAW, New Orleans developer, this old "parking lot for carriages" is now a 12-unit apartment. Described in French Quarter guidebooks as "Spanish Stables," building went up in 1834, thirty-one years after cavalry left town. "Probably built by Spanish masons," says Shaw.

RED BRICK ARCHES were entrances for carriages on ground level; drivers slept above. Shaw, who has sold the property, "put in too much money to make a profit but enjoyed the project."

5.
As Any Artist Can Testify, Old Stables and Carriage Houses Make Marvelous Homes

Long before the average person thought of converting a building behind an old mansion where the family carriage was parked, horses were stabled and a driver and stable boy were lodged, working artists were making old carriage houses and stables into studios. (Unlike a garage, a carriage house had to have a high ceiling, so that the artist could install tall windows. And if the building once served as a great house, he could sleep where the coachman was housed, with water and a toilet close by.) Artists who converted carriage houses lived in a good residential district in a home designed by an excellent architect which had beautiful grounds and gardens.

To anyone with an artist's eye, a carriage house or stable is a creative challenge. (Clay Shaw's comment about "enjoying" doing over the New Orleans' livery stable even though "it was my only conversion in the French Quarter that didn't make me money" attests to this.) Today, carriage houses in small communities, where a few prosperous nineteenth-century families lived handsomely, are snapped up by painters, photographers, film-makers and book designers for studio homes. They are preferred by many home buyers to the old main house on an estate, which is difficult to maintain. They can still be found in good condition behind old mansions in small towns where mills or other big businesses have closed down.

In 1924, Grant Wood, Iowa artist, was given studio and living space in a Cedar Rapids coach house behind a mansion-turned-mortuary, which he decorated for owner, David Turner, who became his patron.

Here, Wood did many of his best-known paintings including "Midnight Ride of Paul Revere" (1932) shown without horse. Later, Wood changed ice wagons into bunkhouse-studios at school for artists, made depot into summer studio.

Carriage House on Side Street

On a side street in New Orleans' Garden District stands an elegant home made from an 1848 carriage house behind a Prytania Street mansion in which a Louisiana governor grew up. Now valued at $250,000, it was purchased partly restored in 1932 on a 60 × 129-foot lot for $18,500 and improved by its present owner, Mrs. Thomas M. Terry. Its garden, built around a swimming pool, has been given a permanent cup by the Garden Society.

Originally, painted doors at right end opened to a small tack room and a carriage room, now a study and living room, measuring 20 × 34 feet. Old brick walls, cemented over to prevent crumbling, are 13 inches thick; windows are 10 feet high and more than 125 years old; flagstones were put down in 1848. In the living room, a Sheraton breakfront from London has "Made for Prince Albert" engraved on the lock.

Entrance hall with floor of pink Tennessee marble leads through home's left wing to pool and formal garden.

In the large living room with its celadon green walls, a clean-lined mirrored fireplace, tailored valances over tall drapery-bordered windows, ceiling-high bookcases, and carpeting of rose beige (especially woven so that no seams mar its expanse), choice furnishings please like fine paintings. On the mantel are Meissen china figurines. Bird prints by Gould hang over a Chippendale desk. A pair of Chippendale armchairs are upholstered in their original hand-embroidered tapestry. Above the door leading to the old tack room with its inner wall of Santo Domingo mahogany is the room's original nineteenth-century valance.

Extending the width of the house at the rear is a 38-foot dining room and enclosed porch. Huge panes of glass have been installed between "Garden District iron grillwork" to permit a sweeping view of the garden. There, azaleas, camellias, sweet olives, hibiscus, hydrangeas, and spring bulbs greet the eye.

Owner bought bricks for addition when city tore down car barn that used to house streetcar named *Desire*.

High-ceilinged carriage room (c. 1870) has fabric wallpaper, French embroidered curtains, handsome fireplace, rare antiques.

Old Bricks, Priceless Antiques

In 1946, Mrs. Walter S. Stern bought a brick carriage house for $19,000 not far from Mrs. Terry's home, also in the New Orleans' Garden district. In the next twenty-five years, she added walls, hallways and a patio made with old bricks.

Walk past the redbud tree through the jasmine-bordered front door (in 1950, 32-foot addition) and you enter a brick-paved hallway to pass between great green plants springing out of Chinese porcelain jardinieres. Move on to the living room or library at right, dining room at left, or back to the glassed-in porch (once a lean-to shed) to see collectors' items everywhere. Goddess of Mercy Chinese lamp, Staffordshire Elijah with raven, tiny French porcelain bidet, great English chest, Irish tea table, Swiss stained-glass window, Dutch brass chandelier—blended to harmonize.

In back, a three-tiered limestone fountain from Spain stands in the center of neat beds of crepe myrtle, tulips, daffodils, and boxwood which Mrs. Stern planned with sheets laid on lawn.

Rare antiques are in every room. Mrs. Stern's bedroom, which is on upper floor where stable boys once slept, has antique French walnut bed, fine chests, draperies made with imported fabric and needlepoint seat covers.

From Tack Room and Six Stalls

In Ojai, California, Marie du Var, now of Leisure World, made a 1928 stable into a lovely home with a central living room flanked by bedrooms and baths to the south; and kitchen, laundry, and garage to the north. Second converter, S. J. O'Jack, added a west wing to the south wing, put in a sauna, dressing room, and carport; roofed back porch, defining its 46-foot back length with Colonial columns; made a circular portico entrance supported by columns.

Old Place in Florida

Natives say the big home once served by this carriage house in Jacksonville, Florida, is more than a hundred years old.

Moved and expanded by an enterprising converter fifty or sixty years ago, this old building has a boarded-up stairway. The outline of this is still visible in floor of the bedroom of one of the children of the present owners, Ed and Mary Anne Bratburd. "This kind of thing makes the house more interesting to us," says Mary Bratburd, who worked out a way for the room's seven-foot ceiling to be carried through addition.

Lovers of history, the Bratburds know that their converted carriage house once served as a guest house when the big house on the river belonged to the Eli Lilly family. Marjorie Rawlings once visited where they live and proofread galleys for *The Yearling*, her Florida classic, while a guest.

Not recognized as a "find" even after it had been moved 50 or 75 feet to its new location in a parklike setting of great trees where it was enlarged, the old building had become a wreck when it was purchased by the Bratburds. Romantic and practical, they saw possibilities for elegance in its simple lines. Now they are doing it over as they enjoy Florida living.

Once a 15 × 15-foot carriage house, this building had a stairway a half century ago that led to second floor. Remodelers appreciate problem areas like old boarded up stairway which give character to home.

Present owners believe mantle with workmanship superior to rest of building was moved to house from another.

SEVEN WAYS TO GET A BARGAIN IN A CARRIAGE HOUSE

Ride up and down streets and alleys in a section of town where grand homes reigned between 1850 and 1900.

Find a building that interests you? Get owner's name through neighbor, but don't make offer until you check zoning rules for converting to home on this lot.

Don't be afraid of another converter's mistakes. Water and electricity may be in and you can remove wrong partitions.

No luck in town? Go to rundown horse farm, academy, army post, an old showplace or farm near town. Search for stable there.

Advertise in small-town newspapers within 25 miles radius of where you live. Mention that your conversion will improve overall property values.

Buy without real estate agent who usually doesn't bother to list nonconverted building on small lot, which is all you need.

If possible, buy cluster of buildings. Sell all but carriage house separately by pointing out conversion possibilities—aiming to make enough on sales to bring your house in free.

That this hillside home was hot-dog stand on a corner 15 miles away can't be imagined unless you were there to watch old stand's trip over hill and dale.

One-time stand is living room; screened front porch, deck, bedroom, kitchen and bath are built around core. Fireplace is at far side; outdoor shower is under deck.

Perched precariously on one of highest peaks in Litchfield County, the little cabin stood like this from Thanksgiving till spring. Then, building began.

Old stock-watering place on hill behind cabin site had live spring with big yield from which water could be brought to house by gravity siphon without pump.

6.
Who Would Think of Making a House Out of a Country Stand or Store?

When we decided to move the hot-dog stand (mentioned in preface) to our property, we selected a site high on a hill to take advantage of the view. Still, the place was not so high that we could not bring in water with gravity alone from a place higher up. This would eliminate the need for an electric pump.

We consulted a trucker who had three questions. Could he get permission from the State Highway people to transport the building on a flatbed truck over a lightweight bridge that had a weight allowance of eight tons? (He could, by using a lightweight truck.) Could he get the 11 × 14-foot building through a space fourteen feet wide between two giant boulders on our hillside? (He did, by placing the building the long way on his truck.) Could he find a way to get the building, which was 20 feet high

"Free, if you cart it away," said buyer of Bridgewater corner which had this stand parked on curb. Cost of moving stand 15 miles to new hilltop site: $500.

under wires that were only 18 feet above ground at one intersection? (At his suggestion, we took off the top of the building at the sill and placed the roof peak-side down inside the cabin. Then, he could go under.) He delivered the cabin in the fall for a cost of $500 C.O.D. In spring, we could convert.

We found a mason to build a chimney of cinder blocks along the north side of the cabin wall with fireplace faced with fieldstones from a nearby stone fence. And we found a carpenter with a helper to carry out our building plan. Before summer, they built a bedroom to the south and a kitchen and bath to the west of the main structure. Then they built a deck on stilts to the east and south of the house, part of which we screened for extra sleeping space. By Memorial Day, we were ready to rent.

Present living room was old cabin, which turned out to be chestnut when red paint was scraped off. This is living room; deck and rooms went on front and side.

89

Learning that cabin had been storage place for traps before it was hotdog stand, we furnished and advertised the converted stand as a "trapper's cabin." Find: ocelot skin which we stretched.

Working out a plan for each room in inches, which we carried scales to, we bought range, refrigerator, sink, tub, lavatory, couches, and bed to fit. Always, we thought of what "they" would want.

Trapper's cabin, which paid for itself in seven years, appeals to New Yorkers who appreciate place on hill "where the air is good to breathe."

School bus, purchased for $375 by artist who rents cabin, serves as work shed and summer studio. It can go with artist to next home.

Our stand was given to us, we had land for a site, construction costs were lower when we put up our cabin than now. So we spent less than you will spend. Still, you may be interested in what we paid out.

Moving of building	$ 500.00
Excavating, putting up temporary blocks (and later support beams)	322.40
Gravel for low spots in trail leading up hill	65.35
Carpentry and materials for additions, roofing, deck	3,625.46
Mason's charge for fireplace and chimney	375.00
Interior work (carpentry, cabinets, roll doors, lumber, hardware)	681.75
Piping in water from spring	495.90
Septic tank and leaching field	871.00
Painting and painter for out and in	156.67
Insurance for $9000 coverage on building and $1000 on furniture	58.00
Gas appliances and furniture from tag sales	450.00
Total	$7,601.53

First summer, we rented cabin for $800, reserving right to enclose pipes under porch and install heater to prevent winter freeze. Then, we advertised for year-round renter at $1000.

Each time a renter moves out, we raise the rent for the next, in line with our higher insurance cost (the cabin is now appraised and insured for $20,000), a higher real estate tax (once clumped with other farm buildings, cabin is now taxed separately at more) and an increased demand by New Yorkers for weekend places. In 1973, we got 26 replies from this ad, which we ran in *The New York Times* on a snowy midwinter Sunday:

RENTALS—CONNECTICUT
New Milford—Converted trapper's cabin (completely f'nshd w/massive fplc) on high peak where air is good to breathe. Avail May $2000 year. (203) 354-3103.

We rented the first afternoon to an artist and his wife who drove 79 miles in a hurry to sign up first. Our tenants are happy and we make a good profit on our converted hot-dog stand.

Like artist in our cabin, Mrs. Bernice Mittower of Republic, Ohio, has roomy bus in yard. She has made it into a postmark museum, which she takes to conventions.

In 1900, the year in which Mrs. Cecil Lewis of Earlham, Iowa, was born, her grandfather, C. D. Bricker, put up this general store.

Seventy years later, Mrs. Lewis, who lived in California, returned to Iowa to make this home out of the old store and the offices above.

Grandfather's Store Becomes Home

Many who are retired dream of going back to their old home town and finding a comfortable house close to the library, post office, church, stores, and old friends. Such a retiree was Mrs. Cecil Lewis, a former buyer for the Navy, who was widowed after living for most of her adult years in California. But instead of going back to the little Iowa town where she was born and fixing up a house, she returned to the Main Street store which had been owned by her grandfather and father and made it into a spacious home.

Downstairs in the building which measures 145 feet from the front door to the garage, Mrs. Lewis has a 40-foot living room (with greenery in the show windows where everything from school tablets to baked goods were once displayed) and dining-room area where she often entertains. Behind is 9 × 20-foot den, 9 × 20-foot kitchen, two bedrooms, laundry, bath and shower. Upstairs, reached by elevator now because "I remembered those thirty steep steps to the second floor from way back when," she has several bedrooms, baths and sitting rooms for guests who like to come to this wonderfully different home right smack in the middle of a little town 29 miles from Des Moines.

An earnest collector of early Americana, Mrs. Lewis has space in room after room to display what she has inherited from her midwestern forebears and found in antique shops, auctions, and galleries. On the wall of her den, she has one of the world's largest collections of horseshoes; in cupboards surrounding one upstairs fireplace, she has a rare collection of antique glass; in all rooms are family treasures. There is a rosewood piano, shutters brought from a great-grandfather's house in a neighboring county, signed Tiffany lamps, a great hutch made by a grandfather who was a cabinetmaker in Muscatine, a collection of iron toys that belonged to her husband as a boy. All are worked into the overall decorative scheme.

Ladder on track is nostalgic reminder of days when clerks climbed to upper shelves where long underwear was stored.

Exterior molding has been repaired, trim is a delicate blue and Austrian shades cover windows.

Carpenters took out old counters and shelves, put up 8-foot partitions to enclose windowless kitchen and powder room on one side, den with fireplace on other. Enclosures get light from big front windows.

Elevator goes now from main floor to second where small town's professional men once had offices and storekeeper stored flour, sugar, salt in bulk which came to the store "by the carload."

The floor plan below shows how rectangular space on lower floor was partitioned off in sections so that owner could have pleasant rooms without making a major change. And it explains how upstairs space was divided into rooms. The picture at upper left shows how ceiling was dropped to accommodate recessed lighting.

The only overspending in the house, according to Mrs. Lewis, went for the elevator which "should have been bought installed." Explaining that she bought equipment from one source, lumber from a builder, electricity from another, the owner says she "paid $3500 for a job that should have cost $2500." Still, she was grateful for her elevator a few months after she had completed her remodeling job and fell and broke her hip. "I couldn't do without it," she says; "and did you notice, it has a phone inside. That's a state law."

Mrs. Lewis says that friends say "You could have built a new house for what you spent on doing over the store." She smiles. "And maybe that's true, but I wouldn't

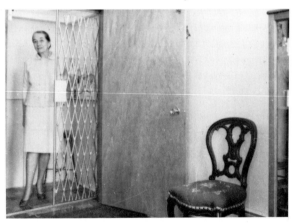

have had as much fun or had anything this well built. My grandfather put up this place, and he knew construction."

With seven or eight rooms downstairs and just as many up, which Mrs. Lewis keeps up with the help of an occasional cleaning woman, many a visitor asks, "Why bother?"

"Maybe I won't someday," answers the owner, who knows that she could turn her two floors into a small apartment for herself with two or three more to rent. "But right now this is just what the doctor ordered."

When Mrs. Lewis' husband died in California the same year that she retired from an active business life, she felt lost. Then, taking the advice of her doctor, who said, "You need a project," she returned to Iowa and bought the building her grandfather had owned for $8000 from family heirs. Ever since, she has been hard at work. "And I've never been sorry."

You have only to watch Mrs. Lewis doing needlepoint in her grandmother's chair, upholstered in soft rose velvet, taking a niece upstairs to see the figurines she found at an Omaha antique store to add to her collection, or pouring tea for a civic group in her living room, and you know that she speaks from the heart. Back on Main Street in her old home town, she is fulfilled.

In her modern 9 × 20-foot kitchen, Mrs. Lewis has shelves for pictures of relatives who stop often to see what's happening at the store.

Bedspread in upstairs room is handwoven, cupboards came by covered wagon from Indiana, silhouettes are of ancestors.

"When I moved in," says Mrs. Lewis, "people thought I planned to open a shop. But my collecting, like the remodeling, is personal."

Known as "Mammy's Cabin" at antebellum plantation in Georgia's Stone Mountain Park, cabin actually was built by old-time doctor for home, office, and drugstore.

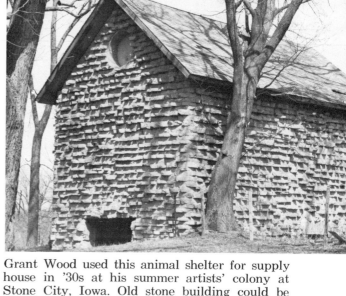

Grant Wood used this animal shelter for supply house in '30s at his summer artists' colony at Stone City, Iowa. Old stone building could be great start for home.

Zebra cabin, which has white stripes of batten over cracks between boards, was built by Georgia slaves in 1850s. It belongs to student who studies beside fireplace.

"Free—if you take it away," says owner of bunkhouse, who is making over old boys' camp as country place. Such buildings are worth moving for housing start.

This 1857 cookhouse under giant magnolia tree behind old white house near University of Georgia became child's playhouse in 1910; now a studio home for musician.

Tiny boathouse on Connecticut lake is used by crew at private school as storage place for gear. Small place like this is worth moving or converting. See country stand, page 88.

7.
Start with One Small Building and You Have a Hideaway

Want a place to go weekends? Instead of looking for land with a vacation cottage, buy raw land with a spring and then look around for a small building that you can move to your selected site. You will save money on lumber and labor, and you will have a place to stay in as you build weekend place.

We have moved and enlarged three buildings. First was the hot-dog stand, described previously, which became the core room for a cottage. Another was a railroad station, which we put on a hill, excavating underneath. Third was a 9 × 30-foot structure which we made into bedrooms, adding this 16 × 24-foot living room.

Original structure looks like log cabin.

Beginning cabin, which we bought for $300 from a Roxbury builder who had used it for temporary living as he put up home, has siding made with 2×8-foot planks, half-rounded and stained dark to look like logs. (Planks were tongue-and-groove, weather-sealed to a single-wall construction of long, low structure.) Narrow building is only 9 feet high and presented no moving problem for the trucker, who charged only $350 for hauling 20 miles.

Situated downhill from converted hot-dog stand, this house can get water from the same spring. Placed on cement-block piers, it became bedrooms and bath for lodge.

Addition has simulated log siding to match.

Unscreened portion of deck juts into trees.

Movers placed the first 9 × 30-foot structure on piers to face east where the screened porch, planned for the front of 14 × 12 bedrooms, could get the morning sun and have a view of the valley. We built the living room at an angle so that the front window could face north for good light. Then we put the kitchen next to the bath between the two buildings to serve both screened porch and dining area in the south end of annex. We planned a no-step approach to the front door near the parking place. As we worked, we built for future winterizing, if wanted.

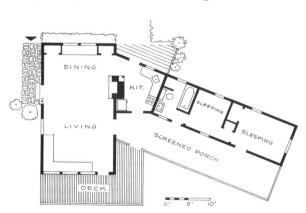

We built the living room wall with 4 × 4-inch vertical studs every 4 feet. (Later, we could put in standard-size sheets of Styrofoam insulation and wood panels.) To the rafters above, we nailed self-insulating fiberboard roof decking which we painted white inside, shingled outside for roof. We insulated the bedrooms and bath and walled with Sheetrock, putting thermostatically controlled heaters in bathroom.

At first, we brought spring water aboveground through 150 yards of plastic pipe, extending from another that fed our cabin higher up. This meant draining each fall. Later, we buried the pipe 3½ feet in the ground (below the Connecticut frost line) and changed the summerhouse to year-round place.

Due to advance planning of all workmen, winterizing (including cost of digging trench to bury pipe) was only $900. This was a good investment. A year later, we were collecting $1000 a year more from a new year-round tenant than we had taken in from our summer renter.

99

Open the door and you see what city escapees
like. A ceiling-high fireplace, long screened-in
porch and view of the woods beyond. Hardwood
floors, cut native stones, and dark beams give
place a substantial look.

Back wall of living-room fireplace made of old bricks became side wall for kitchen, which has built-in barbecue. Steel pipe supports corner of opening (right) for fitted grate and separate flue.

Creative carpenter who laid hardwood floors made cupboards out of tongue-and-groove siding which he stained with wash of gray. He suggested Colonial L & H hinges and donated old door.

We made chandelier by hanging old wagon wheel (with shortened spokes) from block and tackle. Then, we hung Tiffany-type lamp. Table and benches from our design are pine, stained walnut.

Cost of house before winterizing was $11,000 in the middle '60's before inflation sent lumber and labor sky-high. Even then, this was a good price because it included the purchase of a 30-foot cabin, trucking fees, lumber, materials and masonry for chimney and fireplace ($700), screens, glass, furnishings, and bringing in water from a spring. (Again, as with the hot-dog stand, we were fortunate to have water and a good site on the property we had already purchased.) Cost of the place after winterizing was about $12,000.

Because we live near New York where weekend and vacation places are much in demand, we have never been without a renter since the first time we advertised. In the beginning, our tenant paid $1200 a summer; then we winterized and our next tenant paid $2200 for the year. Since then, as our taxes and insurance premiums have gone up, so has the rent. Whatever the price, we always have a waiting list, and the house has long since paid for itself.

Servants' Quarters Becomes
Glamorous Duplex for Mother

When Mrs. Barton Loomis moved from her Boston townhouse to New Orleans to be near her daughter and family, she paid her son-in-law $35,000 for the servants' wing of his 1870 mansion and remodeled it into a tiny but exquisite two-floor apartment.

The wing, which originally was the old cookhouse and laundry, had a stove, soapstone sink, outdoor toilet, and a wooden staircase leading from the courtyard to the second floor. For several years it had housed only heating and air-conditioning units.

With the help of architect Myrlin McCullar, Mrs. Loomis took down the old steps and cleared the place out, making space for a living room, dining area, galley kitchen downstairs, two bedrooms and bath above.

Like a specially built condominium, the wing belonging to Mrs. Loomis is completely self-contained. Heated with natural gas, it has its own unit separate from the house and its own air-conditioning system.

Turned stairway replaces outdoor steps that led to "sleeping stalls for servants who slept over." Glazed antique white walls, molding, rail and panels of pine are "typically New Orleans."

102

When Mrs. Loomis steps through her neat white door with its green-black shutters to her balcony, she looks through the branches of a golden rain tree across a brick courtyard to a swimming pool. This was her gift to her grandchildren, who sometimes come to sit in the miniature ice-cream chairs on her veranda and have a soda.

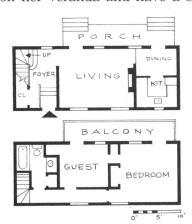

Floors inside are oak, stained walnut. Sheer eggshell curtains are French embroidered. Panels and moldings scaled to fit her 12 × 14-foot living room and 8 × 6-foot dining area are look-alikes for Louisiana's best. The wood-burning fireplace is cypress faced with slate.

Standing in her dining room near the doors that were brought from a ceremonial Japanese tea house is a copy of a small handsome Ming horse. Above is a French chandelier made of gilt wrought iron. One English corner cupboard in her living room was sent to China for decorating.

Happy in her home, the owner explains that if the children sell, she has first refusal rights. "That is for my protection, not that I want to buy." She says she has no desire for a large place. "This suits me." Mrs. Loomis has taken care of that.

More Than One Remodeler Has Started with a Garage

In 1937, Ed Lindig, maintenance foreman for the New York Port Authority, paid $600 for 1½ wooded acres in Brookfield, Connecticut, which has proved to be an excellent investment. He and his wife camped on the land until their first baby came; then Ed put up a garage for use as a bunkhouse until he could build a house. No car was ever parked there. The garage became a small house, then a large one. Finally, when his children and house were grown, Ed built a garage.

First expansion came when Ed added entryway, screened porch and kitchen at front, side and rear of regulation garage. House, which had artesian well, soon had oak floor over original poured cement.

House that Ed built from ground up, with occasional help, has living and dining rooms, kitchen, kitchen, laundry, two bedrooms, bath, and porch.

Working with his hands is a pleasure for Ed, who now lives in Brookfield since his retirement. He keeps working, is now building fireplace.

Where doors of garage once hung is now window across front of house. Entryway (front right) was added when screened side section went on. This became dining room. Fireplace goes in at right.

Dining room with oak floor has kitchen to rear. Long veranda (through window) has floor of flagstones laid by Ed, who says, "Next, I'll have to screen it." An able carpenter, his steps make sense.

If you live in the city and like to work with your hands, follow Ed Lindig's plan for a weekend place. Using garage (A) as bunkhouse with outdoor toilet and cookout place, build on kitchen (B) and bath as first step. Then add screened porch (C) as bedroom, to be used later as dining area. Then add bedrooms (D), and finally add screened porch (E). You will have a good house, even if you never have a garage.

Ed was never extravagant with workmanship or materials. Outhouse became tool shed.

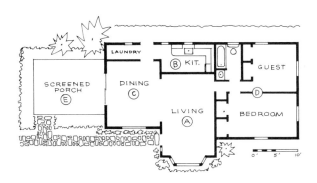

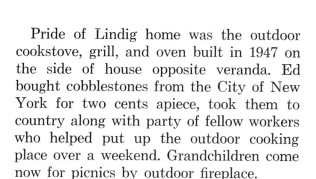

Pride of Lindig home was the outdoor cookstove, grill, and oven built in 1947 on the side of house opposite veranda. Ed bought cobblestones from the City of New York for two cents apiece, took them to country along with party of fellow workers who helped put up the outdoor cooking place over a weekend. Grandchildren come now for picnics by outdoor fireplace.

Would You Buy a Second-Hand Cabin from the Miner Who Owns This Place?

If the price is right, you will, if you are a good judge of lumber, carpentry, and land. So don't let flapping tar paper on a roof and tin over a few windows discourage you from making a good buy. Take away the paper and tin, in this case, and you will find a sound, sturdy building that needs only shingles on the roof and glass in the windows to become the big sitting room for a handsome mountain lodge. Situated near Denver, this rustic home has a long view of the Rockies.

This picture taken in 1900 of a gracious Atlanta home in close-to-business Inman Park proves that early developer, Joel Hurt, understood suburb's appeal. "People like country living where they can commute." By the 1960s, the Victorian mansion had become a tenement, and Hurt's dream suburb was a slum. When designer Robert Griggs bought white elephant, others bought, nearby.

In tenement, a baby slept in drawer of dingy cabinet that had been custom-made of long-leaf pine for room near kitchen. Mice, roaches, and rats lived on shelves behind etched glass.

Before restoration, the house was home for thirty-four members of ten families who paid slumlord a total of $800 a month to live in dingy rooms. Behind poverty, old grandeur persisted.

8.
Biggest Bargain: Old White Elephant that You Can Bring Back to Life

"Bob's folly" is what Georgia friends of Bob Griggs called the monstrous home he purchased for $22,500 on a 100 × 200-foot lot in a rundown section of Atlanta. But take a closer look at the red brick mansion with its beveled windows, fish-scale shingles, and romantic tower. "The bargain of a century," they said.

Is the young designer sorry for the work he let himself in for? "Sometimes," he admits, "I get tired after working half the night. But the next night I walk in and remember what the entrance was like before I put in the stained glass and did over the floors and fireplace and stairway. Then it seems worth the effort."

At Christmas, Bob serves cocktails in drawing room by fireplace which is faced with hand-painted tiles featuring Georgia birds and flowers. Wreaths dramatize honey-colored shutters.

Here, the chandelier, which came with house, is gas. Made of bronze and crystal, it has porcelain candles that can be turned on and lighted one at a time. Victorian pieces came from auctions.

Of all of the old houses put up when Inman Park was new, this one is completely different from the others. Built in 1885 for John Beath, president of the city's ice company, the mansion was a promise to Beath's Yankee bride that if she would come south to live, she could have "the finest home in all Atlanta." Consequently, the mansion has great hinged doors with silver knobs, sinks of pink marble, fireplaces with built-in clocks, windows with panes of stained, beveled, and curved glass with carvings of Cherokee roses and acanthus-leaf capitals in their walnut frames. "At first," says the new owner, "every day I spent in the place was a treasure hunt."

Bob doesn't have to search for the right chandelier, sofa, or marble-topped table for every room. "The stuff jumps out at me at sales, and I can always find a place for the iron toy, rug, or andirons that someone brings from an old attic." His friends and clients have become interested and bring unusual pieces.

A detail-minded man, the owner has replaced every broken tile and mirror in his eight fireplaces and restored every prism and arm in the magnificent chandeliers that hang above polished tables in room after room. His stunning home recently brought a $75,000 offer, but Bob was too busy to think about selling.

With his feeling for color, designer Griggs gets out a red tablecloth for Christmas and pours red wine into crystal glasses. He sets table with Imari porcelain and Wedgwood tureens.

At the left, a pink marble sideboard gleams with nineteenth-century silver, cut glass, and Victorian candelabrums. Draperies, fireplace tiles, chair, and rug are green; garlands contain apples.

On the rainy November day when Bob first saw his house, he had driven to Inman Park to appraise some stained-glass windows in the home of a client who had been warned that a highway was coming through. "We were driving back when I saw this crazy house. There were junk cars in the yard and a "Furnished Apartments" sign in the window, but I stopped and went up to the front door, which was open.

"Children in bare feet were playing in the cold hall where leaves were blowing around. In the dining room a woman was peeling collards. I looked at the carved frames of her windows covered with plastic curtains and said everything was beautiful. She just shook her head."

Before he left that day, Bob walked up the curving stairway. Passing by the second and third floors, he saw lovely old rooms sectioned off with partitions. "Beds with lumpy mattresses and orange crates filled with dirty clothes were all over the place." But the designer didn't turn back. Finally, he came to the tower room with its view of all Atlanta. "That did it! I knew right then I was going to buy the place. At first, I worried about the neighborhood," says Bob, "but now, a couple of hundred other houses have been bought, and we're all working to save Inman Park, the only nineteenth-century area left in Atlanta."

Bob Griggs' library, with its walls above its dark wood paneling covered with red felt, is a festive place for after-dinner coffee, brandy, and cigars, even without the holiday greenery and fruit.

Underneath a bronze chandelier from Savannah, the brass-studded table holds a plum pudding on a silver cake basket. Elizabethan minstrels grace the fireplace; lions' heads are carved in oak.

Once a billiard room, second floor living room has classic fireplace with handsome mirror and wrought-iron base. Scarred pine floor was sanded and painted white like ceiling, molding, and trim.

Williamsburg sheer curtains cover glass in classic windows. Chairs upholstered in leopard-skin fabric look elegant but not heavy, as worked out by owner, whose master bedroom adjoins this room.

As a new graduate of the Atlanta School of Art and beginning decorator and antique dealer, young Bob Griggs had only $2000 when he saw the house he wanted. Assuming three loans taken out by the former owner, he contracted for a fourth, paying back his four loans for the next several years at $170 a month. But of course this was just the beginning.

Biggest expense was for a heating system which Bob bought complete from Sears, paying for furnace, flues, ducts, and radiators long-term at $25 a month. Because of the interest that his relatives, friends, and business associates have taken in his project, his furnishings have not been as costly as they might have been. Many choice items came in as gifts.

Bob has restored room after room with his own hands. "Now, but for the tower and yard," he says, "where I have just set out five hundred tulips, I'm just about done with the back-breaking stuff." He works constantly but does not push, "because I know this big project will take time."

In the beginning, Bob poured epoxy into gutters, sanded and stained or carpeted gouged floors, painted scratched woodwork, repaired gas sconces, fixed up the electric wiring, replaced cracked glass. Later, he turned to decorating. "And that," he says, "has paid off." Bob's home has attracted attention to his decorating talent, so new clients have come to Inman Park where all property, including Bob's home, is now going up in price.

Was This a Yellow Fever Hospital?

In New Orleans there is a fascinating compound of eleven apartments thought by the owner to have been the quarantine house for yellow fever victims in epidemics of 1832 and '34. (Historians say no, the compound was a French military hospital, never used.) Anyway, the brick complex is on land granted to nuns in 1726 by King Louis XV. Now owned by W. Perry Brown, it has won the Vieux Carré Restoration Award. And whatever its past, Brown's apartment is a charmer.

Brick street wall provides protection and privacy.

Open the front door of this bachelor home and you look up a carpeted stairway to a balcony with a wrought-iron railing. Look down and you see a comfortable living room with dining area and bar at the back.

According to public relations man Brown, living room is three to four feet below sea level so drainage system had to be installed under house; walls and floor were treated with epoxy. Now, all's well.

With a minimum of space, Mr. Brown has created a dramatic home that fits his needs in every way. Easy to care for, the lower level has a living room with French doors that open as a window in one wall to let the sun pour in from an outer courtyard. Furnishings against white walls are black. Dining area at the back is small but ample for a formally set table when the occasion demands. To its right is a pass-through bar where guests for most meals can sit on stools to talk with the host, who likes to cook.

There is a long waiting list for one- and two-bedroom apartments with their own patios in the prize-winning compound for which the owner paid $225,000—a bargain price for ten income-producing apartments plus a home. Residents who swim behind this apartment have a camaraderie like that of members in a private club. Mr. Brown's happy-looking home is a natural gathering place for the group.

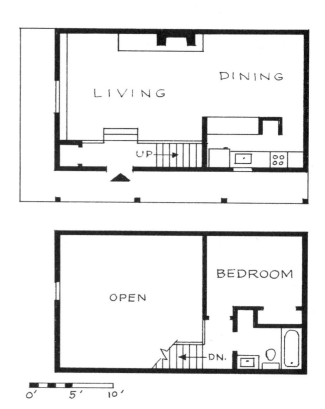

Old bricks for foyer and fireplace became available when 1834 building in French quarter was demolished. Epoxy-covered brick walls and panels are white. Doors and rail are black.

Iowa Congressman Transforms Hotel on Mississippi

On a towering buff, above the town of Mc-Gregor, Iowa, stands a rambling two-story building with a spectacular view of the rolling hills of Iowa and Wisconsin—and, some with keen eyes say, of Minnesota and Illinois, too. Built as a summer hotel in 1922, "The Heights" was purchased in 1969 by Rep. John Culver (Dem.) of Cedar Rapids and his wife, who have transformed it into a home for them and their four children.

"We bought it as a summer place," say the Culvers, who live in Washington, D.C., when Congress is in session, "but we enjoy ourselves here in the fall and at Christmas."

At any season, the Culvers can sit on the glassed-in front porch of their waterfront home where thirty-six "guests" sat down for hotel meals and watch boats go up and down Mark Twain's favorite river.

Hotel changed to mansion on a bluff when owners removed old stairways on downhill side, painted building white. The Culvers took away old sheds, groomed lawn to bluff's edge, added no doodads as they did old place over.

Conversion was a matter of removing ramshackle add-ons (above) rather than a complete revamp job. Note how porch at back was enclosed, one at side was added, big one at front was left "as is." Hotel's upstairs hall and eight bedrooms are now a sitting room, four bedrooms. Fireplace is huge.

The top of the steeple is gone and there is a new doorway. Otherwise, the exterior of the old church in North Salem, New York, is the same as when wealthy parishioners arrived out front in horse-drawn carriages. Long the home of the town postmaster, who purchased the building and furnishings in 1951 for $3000, the church has been changed inside from basement to balcony.

Built in 1870, New Salem's Universalist Church had a forceful pastorate until the 1920s, when the town's personality changed and attendance dwindled. Finally, in 1946, the church was dissolved and the building was sold at a bargain price.

116

9.
Praise the Lord
if You Happen to Find a Church

In 1951, Warren Lucas asked his wife-to-be whether she would like to live in a church. "As a nice Irish Catholic girl, Betty was delighted," says her husband. So after the wedding, he carried his bride over the threshold of an old Protestant church which he had bought complete with pews, collection plates, chancel chairs, organ pipes, stained-glass windows. Now, many years and five children later, Mr. Lucas, who works a few steps away, "wouldn't trade our church for the Vatican."

Starting with a borrowed saw, the Lucases have done all remodeling, turning to professionals only for heavy plumbing and heating.

The downstairs, which had a nave, transept and chancel, has a bedroom and kitchen on opposite sides of the central aisle at the back and a living room up front. Instead of the old organ, there is a piano, and replacing the old arched window at the back are glass doors that open onto an outdoor patio.

Library and bedroom suite for daughters is on balcony which has ceiling of striated walnut. Balustrade has been pieced together from sections of black walnut taken from choir stall.

Glass door was "stained" with paint by Mrs. Lucas, who also scraped and refinished floors, replastered walls, reupholstered altar chairs. L-shaped stairway and lighting are husband's handiwork.

For church atmosphere in entry, the Lucases made chandelier from Catholic incense burner, hung religious plaques sent as gift from convent, and added as medieval touch a suit of armor.

From balcony library, Warren can project movies to screen in room below balustrade. He made "bird-in-cage" stairway leading to boys' suite above from water pipe, steel rods, walnut treads.

Lucases gave pews, pipes, and stained-glass window to Universalist church in nearby town when they remade building which had good basement where church suppers were held. With church came a half acre of land with brook.

In 1869, North Salem's Universalist Society allocated a sum of $7200 for the building of a church within ten months ("from the sills up") on a foundation already laid by the committee. And in 1886, a historian referred to the handsome church as being "valued at about $20,000." Thus, the $3000 paid by the Lucases sixty-five years later is a phenomenon, which the owners appreciate. "And we also appreciate the history of the church," they say, "and so do the children. Living here has enriched our lives."

Old-world elegance is heightened with paintings of harpists, girondelles from other churches, polished mahogany table made from trees brought to Norwalk as ballast, and reupholstered organ bench. Church attracted gifts.

Above the balcony where the three Lucas girls have two bedrooms and living room, the Lucas boys have bedroom, bath, and recreation room. "Here," says mother, "the building's acoustics carry sound up and out. Every mother should be so lucky."

Having spent her married years living in this church, Betty Lucas has naturally been asked whether she has considered what life might have been in a more conventional dwelling.

"The children have enjoyed bringing their friends here, and we have had room to build anything we have wanted into our home as we have gone along." Thoughtfully, she adds, "We might have had as good a life in a more conventional home, but I don't see how it could have been better."

Small Church Becomes Charming Home

To convert church with 25 × 45-foot room, carpenters replaced one wall of 5 × 10-foot coat room on left side of center aisle with new one farther forward, enclosing 10 × 20-foot bedroom. They added tub and shower to 5 × 10-foot toilet room opposite, putting 15-foot kitchen ahead. They left remaining space "as is" for a living room, which has a plant room at right on a platform where there was a dressing room. Laundry equipment is in the basement.

The small house is "just right" for Boyd and Alma Evans, who wanted a retirement place with easy maintenance in a Connecticut village not far from daughter and grandchildren.

Like many small-town churches, this one (Christian Science—c. 1923) was built far back from shady street. Today, with its carpet of grass, mature dogwood trees and place for garden, it is a charming home.

Church now has door opening to platform where readers stood. Raised area with choice furnishings gives character to this compact, easy-to-care-for home.

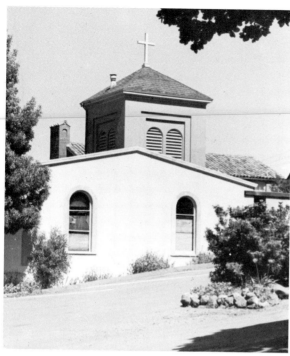

No home on the Italian Riviera is more elegant than this Sausalito church *could be* if converted like one of large barns in this book. Surrounded by walks with wondrous view of water, it has been for sale for $50,000.

Purchased at public sale by Nik Krevitsky, Director of Art for Tucson schools, this Mexican church (now studio-home) on two Arizona acres has 22-inch walls and bell tower. High bid was 10 percent below appraisal.

Investor bought 1859 sandstone church near University of Georgia in Athens for supper club, denied by zoners. Now he rents to students who appreciate home complete with "ghost of baby," buried a century ago under church.

Like many churches in New England mill towns this one in Massachusetts has been boarded up since mill shut down and town's population decreased. Such overlooked buildings often go to outsiders as bargains.

Crumbling adobe walls in Tucson's Catalina foothills were all that were left by 1900 of once prestigious Fort Lowell where eighteen army officers and 239 enlisted men were quartered in 1880s. Abandoned after Geronimo campaigns, buildings costing millions became ruins.

Carved door leads to home converted from old post trader's store, which had gaming rooms and bars for officers and enlisted men. Purchase price in 1935 for store's shell and four acres: $800. Price in 1943 for old commissary was more, but a bargain.

10.
Old Fort Becomes Magnificent Desert Home

Peter and Charles Bolsius, born in Holland in the early 1900s, came as young men to America, where Peter married and migrated with his wife and brother to the Southwest. In Tucson, Arizona, remembering a great territorial-style home in New Mexico, they bought as a start the adobe shell of an old post store. Close but not in Fort Lowell, it had been a place where officers and soldiers gambled and drank.

With no money or building experience, they began to build their dream mansion with a 35-cent chisel and a Mexican helper who could make and lay adobe bricks (at

$50 a thousand). Five years later, they had a rambling 175-foot desert home.

The Bolsiuses planned the interior of their home as they restored old walls. They would make a living room where the post store had its central hall, or *zaguán*, as such entrance rooms are called in the Southwest. They would have white walls and round pueblo-style fireplaces. They began to carve beams and valances for a Spanish effect.

When their home was finished in the '40s, the three Bolsiuses bought the old fort's commissary and built a second home and apartments. Today, their project (with

eighty-five hand-carved doors like the one above) rivals Fort Lowell as an Arizona landmark.

The remodelers put a dining room, kitchen, and sitting rooms to the west where officers had bar and game rooms. And they made bedrooms, baths, and a studio to the east where enlisted men "whooped it up." Many years later, when Mrs. Bolsius

PAGE 124, TOP: *Zaguán* with Spanish door and a tile floor, fireplace, and broad window with view of mountains is impressive entryway and central room.

PAGE 124, BELOW LEFT: There is relief carving in niche of St. Elizabeth of Hungary who turned bread into roses the way the Bolsiuses turned store into home.

PAGE 124, BELOW RIGHT: Bedroom has ceiling made from timbers found along road, carted home and cut by brothers.

ABOVE, LEFT: Beams, beds, chests, and door in guest bedroom were carved by original trio, who also painted flowers.

ABOVE, RIGHT: Bathrooms with whitewashed walls have beamed ceilings, Spanish-type arched doorways leading to showers.

died, Peter remarried, bought his brother's interest in the home, and lived with his second wife in the rooms as pictured and explained here.

Not an authentic restoration, the Bolsius home is more substantial-looking than the old store. Ceilings with great beams cut from timbers found along road or from a torn-down railroad trestle are stronger than the original ones made of mud and cactus sticks (with muslin stretched underneath to catch the dust). Glass walls open up view of flowers planted by the second Mrs. Bolsius, desert and mountains which could not be seen so well through narrow territorial-type windows. Floors of cement blocks and Mexican tiles with Indian rugs are more formal than when soldiers danced.

The place is air-conditioned, of course, and walls of sturdy adobe bricks (made for many rooms by the Bolsiuses, who learned from the natives) are leakproof. Light fixtures which could have been hand-crafted in Mexico but were made by Peter Bolsius out

of popcorn tins are impressive. And the doors, hand-carved, anointed with gasoline and tar and burned in a secret Bolsius antiquing process, are as fine as any made by a Spanish woodcarver. In the opinion of most visitors, "The officers never had it so good."

Dining room was officers' bar in post store, nicknamed "Suttler's store" because of Congressman Suttler's pushing through a bill allowing drinking and gambling 100 feet or more from post after a previous bill had forbidden sale of liquor on army premises. The table is slab of pine on an oak base, carved by the Bolsiuses, who also made arm-chairs, cabinets, doors, and the lustrous tin frame for mirror. Cloth, pottery and candlesticks are Mexican.

The first Mrs. Bolsius' handiwork is seen in kitchen, which has hand-painted shades above custom-made cabinets with splash board of Mexican tile. Brothers' thinking is obvious from floor (poured cement with creases at pressure points to prevent cracking) to ceiling (made with beams salvaged at Redrock, Arizona, when old railroad trestle came down). Plan of house with rambling, random rooms is typical of western territorial homes with rooms that "grew."

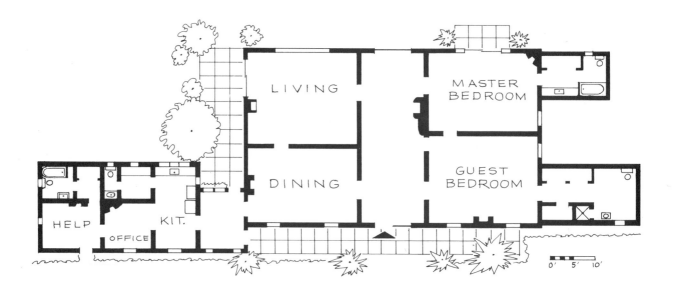

Through Gate to Brother's Home

Old commissary was converted by Charles, who married after the original trio had finished the big house. He furnished the home in Spanish style, like first. Special attention-getter: massive chairs with names of famous guests on back—Dwight Eisenhower, Margaret Sanger, Billy Mitchell, Thornton Wilder, and others.

Bolsius Brothers Worked On and On

The Bolsiuses made quartermaster storerooms into five apartments, which they sold in 1973 for $90,000. One unit, entered through ocatillo gate, is the home of James Sinski, University of Arizona professor.

The living room, which won a national award for good interior design, has red draperies, ceramic coffee table made by Sinski, tiny lights in niches, wrought-iron chandelier with candles dipped to fit. Basic to its great looks are "typically Bolsius" white walls, corner fireplace, dark beams.

GOOD BUYS: MILITARY BUILDINGS NOT YET CONVERTED

Across the road from Fort Lowell's commanding officer's quarters, now restored as museum by Arizona Historical Society, are these adobe ruins, vintage 1880.

Old walled rooms can be made into territorial-type home by someone with down payment for private owner, construction mortgage, vision, taste, and energy.

Send bid for military building like this garage and shop if you own land near post and can transport.

Chapel was sold as bargain at California army camp after Vietnam when soldiers in training went home.

High bidder paid $150 for barracks at Camp Roberts, California, which he dismantled and moved to farm.

District engineer accepts sealed bids for government buildings like this when post says they're not needed.

11.
Talent Grows in a Greenhouse

At Christmas, during a Connecticut blizzard, William and Joan Talbot and their four children sit down for dinner in a grove of fig, palm, and lemon trees. The Yule log in their fireplace burns in a leafy paradise of ferns, rubber plants, and bamboo. Their home in Warren is a greenhouse that even in midwinter is filled with the scent of orange blossoms, oleanders, and roses.

Bright with sunlight in the day, the lush main room is lighted with shafts of soft yellow light from hidden spotlights at night. The healthy indoor foliage is feathery and mysterious.

Knowledgeable about plants, flowers, and trees since boyhood, when he worked for the St. Louis Botanical Gardens, William Talbot can't remember when he didn't want to live in a greenhouse. "I knew a family who made one into a home, and I never forgot how it felt to walk into that place."

An easy gardener who understands the needs of growing things, he gives "just enough" but educated care to his exotic nursery as he has done with his children. He has long encouraged all four, who are vigorous, and blooming, to follow bent.

Sand and gravel floor is raked after meals, not swept, and is sprayed weekly when jungle-thick plants and trees are watered. This creates humidity, controls dust in exotic greenhouse home.

Glass-walled studio in adjoining barn is workshop for sculptor-owner. Picture by friend, Peter Fink, shows Talbot at work on concrete "nuclear" totem which has sound-activated "windows."

131

Greenhouse, warmed by sun, fire, and electric heat, is snug in winter. And it is cool in summer when sides of glass roof are raised like wings. Straw mat across two rafters makes shady bower.

In adjacent barn, Mrs. Talbot has sunlit sewing corner with glass walls and greenhouse feeling.

Nooks are everywhere for family musicians, weavers, potters, cooks, gardeners, and painters.

In family of "creative Talbots," Bill is a sculptor and indoor and outdoor gardener, and Joan teaches remedial reading at Rumsey Hall School and is a creative cook who entertains as many as sixty at impromptu get-togethers. She also sews and weaves. One son, Peter, is an architect; another son, John, is a carpenter; Augusta is an artist already acclaimed by New York critics for her "mixed media sculpture." Constance is a potter who has been studying the work of natives in Peru. All have contributed to the home furnishings, which are not fancy but serviceable and creative.

Bill made candleholders and sconces for the greenhouse out of galvanized metal, flashing and glareless lights out of sheet-metal cones. The boys made the dining-room table out of flagstones mounted on an iron base and the others out of slabs of granite on jardinieres. The girls made huge clay pots for the standing plants, collected cowhide for rugs and woven throws for garden chairs which the Talbots use indoors, and made plaques and paintings for solid walls.

In the spring, glassed-in tropical plants meld with outdoor dogwood trees that are between house and a garden that provides the Talbots with squash, lettuce, and tomatoes. Fragrant herbs in the kitchen blend with that of lilac. Uncaged white doves fly out of a pomegranate tree past a swallow's nest glued to the frame of an outdoor barn door painted red. Result: a natural abundance that is breathtaking in its appeal. The same with indoor-outdoor furnishings.

Polished slabs of granite on hunks of tree trunks or great stone urns are circled around the inexpensive chairs. (Brightened with hand-woven throws, these seats of canvas and wood look exactly right on floors of gravel and flagstones.) Blazing out from a moss-covered wall is a Talbot sculpture; overhead is a spotlight cut from a coffee can; on a panel of chestnut, an antique Greek rug hangs next to an abstract painting; growing out of a Peruvian pot made by Constance is a vigorous-looking tropical tree with real bananas.

Stay at the Talbot house five minutes and the telephone rings, a neighbor comes, children laugh. Everything is *alive.*

Next time you go into a greenhouse, stand for a minute in the midst of the dense, moist greenery and think of making this place into a combination living and dining room. If you are tantalized with the thought of enjoying a Caribbean environment all day every day, stay on the lookout for a greenhouse that is selling out and can be converted on the spot. (Or, perhaps, can be moved to your land.) *Or* build a greenhouse as an addition to your home. Eventually, as at the Talbots', this greenhouse addition will be the most popular room in your home.

This ore-processing mill or tipple was built about 1860 after a party of Georgia prospectors found yellow metal near "Georgia Gulch" in Breckenridge, Colorado. Tower is now seven-floor home.

Living room entered from long deck has terra-cotta tile floor, pine-paneled walls, support beams of spruce. Furniture is Spanish mission, counter-top is Mexican tile, view is Colorado spectacular.

12.
In Colorado Mining Tipple, Everyone Has a Suite

More than $100 million in gold came out of Breckenridge in its boom days, but the old Colorado mining town was a ghost place by the 1960s when United Airlines Captain Leslie Holtz bought this tipple.

All the time that Holtz, a bachelor, was rebuilding floor after floor of the tower, skiers from Denver, sixty miles to the east, were looking forward to winter weekends in Breckenridge. (West of the Continental Divide, the village was unapproachable in bad winters.) In 1970, sportsman David Lowe, president of a Denver advertising agency, and his wife saw the tower and made Holtz an offer, which he accepted. By 1973, Straight Creek Tunnel had been cut through the Divide, Breckenridge was booming as it hadn't boomed in a hundred years, and the Lowe family of six, all enthusiastic skiers, were living in a seven-floor tipple with space on each floor for a suite.

Climbing up the side of a mountain, the tower's central stairway rises 92 feet. Supported by a criss-cross of 10 × 10-foot beams (mortised and pegged or bolted together), the steps have a steel cable from a nearby ski lift as a handrail.

Above the main floor, on six different levels, members of the Lowe family have bedrooms, sitting rooms, saunas, libraries, playrooms, study rooms, billiard rooms, bunk rooms, game rooms, and studios. Except for the second-floor master bedroom and sauna suite, which is papered, all rooms are wood-paneled. Floors are tiled, carpeted, or have wide boards, and giant exposed support beams are everywhere. Great doors, brought from Mexico, close off some rooms.

Walk from the long main deck through sliding glass doors to the living room and you enter a world that is neither rough-hewn nor polished but the best of both. Beams are spruce timbers, stained satiny brown. Tables, chairs, and sofa from Mexico are massive and hand-carved. Blowing snow seen through glass windows is balanced inside by two snow-white walls. The Mexican tile floor is organic-looking but gleams.

Go past the kitchen up the central stairway and you come to the master bedroom with white-paneled walls, an enormous bed with a hand-carved headboard, closets with doors brought from Mexico, a sauna with sophisticated wall covering separated from toilet and tub by a huge beam. Child's room is on the same level, and a few steps up is son's bedroom and project room encased in a webbing of beams. Next floor is a sitting room and bedroom for one of the younger girls, and above that are two floors of guest

suites complete with beds, reading and writing places, lookout benches and baths. On the sixth floor is a recreation room with bar, pool table, guitars, record players, comfortable chairs and couches. And finally, on the seventh floor is a tower room for the Lowe's oldest daughter, who goes to school in the East but comes to stay during the holidays in her private loft with its awe-inspiring view of the Rockies.

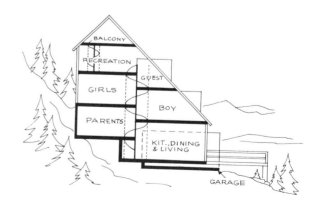

Changing from bachelor's log cabin to tower for vital couple with four children called for doors on bedrooms, studies, TV rooms on floors that had been open. Child's room went in next to the parents' suite, and the loft went up on top of the tipple as a homecoming place for daughter away at school. All rooms become purposeful, as shown and described here.

GREAT STAIRWAY (below) encased with beams in central shaft has steps (with cable handrail) that wind around pole and have seven stopover places on way to tower.

OPEN KITCHEN (below right) has big refrigerator, two ovens, butcher table and tiled counter for easy meals.

MASTER BEDROOM (above kitchen) has view of mountains, carved bed, elegant wallpaper, adjoining sauna and bath.

BOY'S ROOM (above parents') gains drama from view of mountains, beams around stairs. "Project room" adjoins.

RECREATION ROOM (top right) on sixth level has pool table, bar, TV. With balcony on 7th, it is ideal place for young guests whose noise can't disturb parents.

137

13.
Every Hour Is Recess Time
in a Schoolhouse Right for You

"RECESS" says the sign on pole, and what better name for a weekend place that once was a schoolhouse? Tucked away in shady places on by-ways in Pennsylvania, New Jersey, upper New York State, and Connecticut (where this schoolhouse is located) are dozens of such conversions. Purchased as cast-off for a few thousand (and sometimes for a few hundred) dollars in countless counties wtih new consolidated schools, the old one-roomers have been changed into homes that make the "house tour" list right along with remodeled Colonials.

Most schoolhouses are sturdily built and made to withstand heavy weather. All are near a spring or have a well nearby. Some that once had outhouses have been "modernized" and have indoor toilets adjoining girls' and boys' cloakrooms. Some have furnaces; most have electricity and are on passable roads; all have good light from many windows. Also, due to America's salute to Arbor Day, they usually have trees.

In the East, an occasional schoolhouse comes up for sale in Vermont, New Hampshire, or Massachusetts, but most are second-time-around buys. If the building hasn't been converted, this can be a good buy, but in the Middle West the buys are better. There, where conventional home-buyers are not concerned about inner-city problems, and not looking for off-beat buildings, a country schoolhouse can go unnoticed for years. Make an offer, and you will get a bargain.

A few years ago, a dozen schoolhouses were offered for sale north of Minneapolis for $100 apiece. Farther south in Iowa, we bought one with two floors for $1600. Later, when we couldn't get out to redo the building as planned, we resold (*with our remodeling plan*) at a profit on a long-term contract which brings a higher interest rate than we could get from a bank. The secret of our sale was *the plan*. Many who appreciate a bargain refrain from buying because they don't know what to do with the place. One converted schoolhouse near us (below), lived in by widowed sisters who attended the school as children, is built on the bank of a rushing stream where one of the residents "used to swim after school." Such idyllic sites are not uncommon.

Built in 1897 on land donated by a Connecticut farmer who wanted his six children and others in district to have a good education, schoolhouse was remade years later by daughter, Anna.

Anna's old schoolroom is living room with bathroom and stairway behind pine cupboards. Bricks for fireplace came from school chimmey; oak flooring is original. Cloakrooms are now bedrooms.

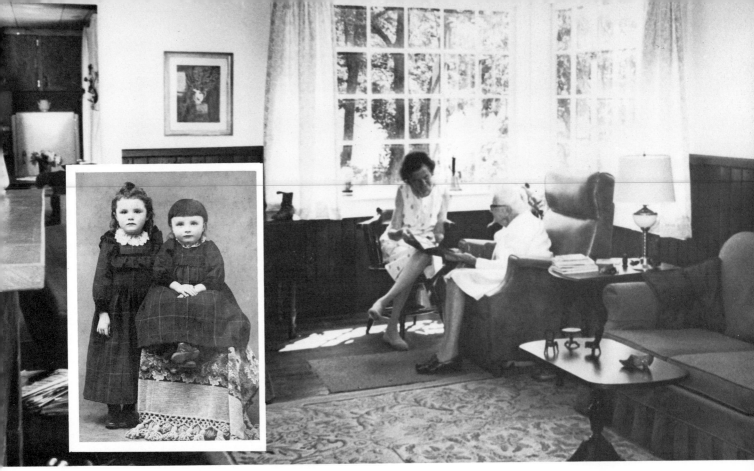

Little girls when their father gave land, Anna and her sister Marian went through school's eight grades. At auction years later, Anna and her husband bought school and acre for $2500.

Now widowed, Anna and Marian live together on acre where they once picked strawberries, waded in brook, planted tamaracks—now giant trees. They can see from here where they were born.

The door at center front between two coatrooms to main schoolroom was blocked off so coatrooms could be enlarged for bedrooms. Entrance is now at the side, to right of annex, which contains kitchen. Living room with fireplace and large bathroom that serves two bedrooms take up most of school's original space. The stairway goes up to an extra bedroom and storage space on gabled second floor.

The school's old outhouses are gone, but a small house that held wood for school's potbelly stove serves as tool shed. Neat black shutters and old cupola that held the school's bell give Anna's restored schoolhouse a well-groomed but jaunty look. Complete conversion—outdoors and in—$12,000.

Old Schools Sold with Coming of New

In 1959, in Gardenville, Pennsylvania, Plumstead Township's school board announced that its eight country schoolhouses would be sold at auction. Above is a commemorative plate with pictures of the old schools and the new consolidated, and on this page and the next are two of the buildings, now remodeled.

Purchaser of the Gardenville School (top center on plate) was Frederick Rarig, lawyer, professor, and farmer, who paid $7900 for a handsome stone building on one-half acre of land which once had belonged to the 170-acre farm where he was now breeding cattle. The buyer of Rocky Ridge School (bottom center on plate) was Charles V. Swain, antique dealer, art historian, and member of the American Institute of Interior Design, whose high bid was $7100.

Father of four, Frederick Rarig used stone schoolhouse until '73 as woodworking shop and for parties and meeting places for professional groups. Now, $30,000 conversion includes annex of polished mahogany.

A few years ago, Mr. Swain sold his converted schoolhouse to Robert Harnett of Philadelphia who has added two extensions, one of which is at the back where there is now a swimming pool.

Central room of home serves as sitting place and entrance hall with living room to right, dining room and kitchen to left. Bedrooms and bath are upstairs. Furnishings are choice.

Mr. Swain, who now lives in a beautifully restored home on 130 acres at Doylestown, did not want the schoolhouse he purchased at the Plumstead sale to look like a schoolhouse, but he did want a sturdy-looking early American home as a background for his Colonial antiques. As architect and interior designer, he planned and supervised work done by professional builders who removed the belfry and placed a massive chimney at each end of the main structure. (One of these accommodated the furnace; the other was purely decorative; a third one on the new wing was for the real fireplace.) *Including the original cost of the building and landscaping*, Mr. Swain spent $41,000 for his schoolhouse home (converted in ten months) where he lived for several years.

A perfectionist, Mr. Swain planned each inch of his house with his furnishings in mind. One wall in the dining room, known as the "pewter room," was made of old shutters which were stripped, refinished, matched and balanced before installation. The mantelpiece and wall paneling were copied from an eighteenth-century home.

HOW TO BUY A SCHOOLHOUSE

When discontinued schools are auctioned, they are sold at public sale by an auctioneer who seeks increasingly high bids until no one overcalls, or they may be sold by sealed bid to high bidder. Before sale day, a minimum price for each building is announced, and bidding starts there. Minimum is low, because appraiser evaluates what is there (not possibilities you can see), and no real estate broker is involved. So you can get a bargain unless another bidder competes.

When you admire an abandoned school, call tax assessor in nearest town and ask who owns it. If district hasn't sold, call school superintendent (whose name you can get from town clerk) and ask if school has been appraised and is for sale. Offer minimum.

When building has been built with town funds, but the land underneath has simply been "loaned" by farmer, you will have to buy and move schoolhouse or buy school and land from two parties. Get broker to help if you don't know the town. He gets a small commission but collects from two.

Want an unusual and *secure* home in a city near your work? Buy your town's jail. Or if this seems far out, look around for another well-built building no longer serving its original purpose. Good buy right now: a filling station. See in this chapter what another has done.

14.
Finds for City Dwellers: Jails, Filling Stations, Basements, Garages, and Firehouses

Creative people in cities are converting warehouses, firehouses, substations, boat docks, garages, filling stations, *and even jails*, which for obvious reasons are well built.

In Perrysburg, Ohio, Mrs. Charles W. Hoffman, long interested in history and antiques, has bought one of the four buildings in the Toledo area listed in the National Park Service's Register of Historic Places. It's the old Wood County Jail, now converted to three apartments with its authenticity preserved.

The architect for the building (built when Polk was President) received $15 for his plans and for supervising construction. Costs, which included the making of small hand-made bricks for four interlocking walls, added up to $2150. The jailer and his family received free residence and 75 cents per day for each prisoner

Seven sheriffs lived and worked in the old jail before the county seat was moved to Bowling Green in 1870. Besides his housing allowance for prisoners, the sheriff was paid 37½ cents per day for apprehending them. He could also turn in an expense account for shackles, medical expenses ($3 for the year 1854) and cordwood ($6.50 for 13 cords in 1857). No sheriff lived in the jail during the latter part of the nineteenth century, although the building continued to house an occasional lawbreaker until 1899, when the new town hall was built with two portable cells behind the mayor's office. The old jail stayed "as is" until recently.

Entrance to 8 × 30-foot living room, once jail's bullpen, has iron latticework door weighing 400 pounds. Closets, once 4 × 6-foot cells, have similar doors. Key-locked stone wall has cannonballs in blocks. Ceilings are reinforced concrete.

Carpenters found a rusty hacksaw blade hidden in a plaster crack, but the prisoner must have been a dreamer. Walls and floors of the old bullpen and cells are made of cut stones (3 × 2 feet thick) with reinforced masonry between stones. (As researched by Perrysburg's *Bend of the River* magazine, hemispheres were cut into the top and side of each stone block and cannonballs were inserted to form a network.

Above cells in old days was a barred room for mentally ill. In Ohio jail, this "lunatick" room is now an attractive apartment, as is jailer's quarters which has walls made of walnut planks held together with iron rivets.

Sarasota station was dirty and rundown when retired engineer saw "For Sale" sign and checked city's assessment ($16,270). Paul Entrekin bought for Texaco's $13,000 asking price.

Station's old office is owner's downtown office and library where he reads, talks to friends, and thinks through personal projects as he once concentrated at desk at Bethlehem Steel.

"The car-lift area makes a good studio," says owner, who works at drawing board every morning, "because the ceiling is high." Indirect light comes from suspended tubes recommended by Environmental Health and Research.

Filling Station Becomes Studio

"Things usually work out," says Paul Entrekin, long-time vice-president and director of Bethlehem Steel Corporation, "if they are well thought through before work is begun." Mr. Entrekin, who is seventy and retired, began planning at fifty-seven what he would do when his business years ended. Through reading, observing and working, he taught himself to do metalworking, woodworking, and painting. Now each morning he leaves the handsome apartment he shares with his wife in Sarasota, Florida, and goes to a downtown studio where he concentrates on his new interests the way he concentrated on the steel business as a young mining engineer. "And I'm enjoying life more than ever," he says.

Typically, Mr. Entrekin's studio is no community room where he splashes through the day with carefree dabblers. Nor is it a rented loft where he is all alone. His downtown work place is a former filling station, remodeled at a cost of $10,000 to include a studio where its owner paints and has a small refrigerator and hot plate if he wants lunch; a library where he reads, enjoys his friends, and works at his desk; a toilet; and a woodworking room where he can frame his paintings. How this all came about when Mr. Entrekin was in his seventieth year is worth considering by all who think life ends at a farewell retirement office party.

By the time he was sixty-five, Mr. Entrekin's paintings (mostly acrylic) were attracting attention at juried shows in Florida. He began taking lessons and worked seriously in a rented studio in Siesta Key. Later, he looked for a studio closer to home and found it on a triangular 135 × 119-foot lot between two busy streets a block from Sarasota's center.

He agreed to pay $13,000 asking price for the station, paying $1000 to be held in escrow until delivery of the deed. He knew how he wanted to convert when title guarantee came through.

Studio has new arbor, wall, and air-conditioning and heat units in 3 × 4-foot annex. Building was sanded and sprayed with Sacreete; termite-ridden timbers were replaced.

One toilet was taken out to enlarge library, paneled in American cedar plywood painted white. Books line two walls; toilet and woodworking shop open off room; heater is at north end.

Woodworking shop, where owner frames paintings, has new wood floors, pegboard walls, and suspended, well-insulated ceiling (here and in studio) with ducts above. Old plumbing and wiring has been renewed.

Owner can fix sandwich and coffee with toaster and hot plate and keeps cold drinks in refrigerator for friends who come to discuss art and current events. Still, he uses station for work, not as guest house.

Not all of Mr. Entrekin's day is spent at the drawing board, although he stays at the studio from morning until five or six o'clock at night. "It's a good place," says the owner, "to read, go over my mail, look out the window and philosophize with friends who come in." Having shunned publicity most of his life, Mr. Entrekin let us tell his story, believing it may interest retired persons as well as remodelers.

Not everyone, he knows, will want to do over an old filling station, "but it does make an ideal studio and presents few problems you can't anticipate." Two problems Mr. Entrekin knew he might have and did something about were termites (he drilled holes in sills and around building, killing termites with chemicals pumped in under pressure) and a possible explosion (he filled old gasoline tanks with water so no gas could collect). Conversion brought no surprises.

Mr. Entrekin's talent for "dreaming something up, laying it out and developing it" shows in his paintings, say judges, as it does in his remodeling. "It's obvious in his entire life-style," friends say. (He planned his home, made from two apartments with a spectacular view, around his and his wife's art interests.) He thinks things through.

His studio, which he changed from an unkempt filling station to a quiet retreat behind a neat wire-mesh fence, belies the insistence of many that "all the good buildings are gone." There are filling stations to be done over everywhere.

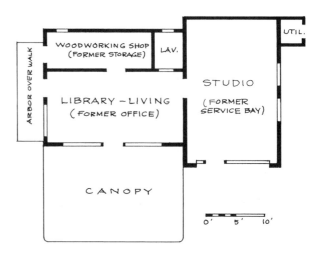

My Sister Eileen
Never Had It So Good

When Rosalind Russell and Edie Adams wept in their city basement in *My Sister Eileen* about why-o-why-o-why-o they ever left Ohio, they never thought of doing the place over as a contemporary cave as Art and Trudy Detrich have done in Chicago.

Art's father, an industrial exhibit designer, told his son he could have the basement of a two-flat building he owned "to create his own living environment." Art planned arched doorways leading to and from room-sized spaces with rounded walls and curved windows. He covered the walls with lath wire curved to suit, coating with a gray structural fibrous plaster. Finally, he hired a plasterer to cover this inner structure with textured white plaster. He hid the gas meter with a painting, covered old radiators with filigree.

Except for actual plastering, Art Detrich, Chicago audio-visual producer, did all work that changed dark northside basement into contemporary home for himself and his wife. Artists call apartment "flowing tunnel of space."

Cost of remodeling, including labor and materials, was $7500. Biggest outlay went for purple shag rug that runs along floors and curves up on walls ($1200) and for plastering over Art's curved wire laths ($1700).

Guests pull up tall chairs to leatherlike counter for beef Stroganoff prepared by Judy Detrich, dental hygienist, guitarist, and gourmet cook. Range in kitchen hides building's furnace, rolls out on casters.

Three black vinyl beanbags serve as chairs in living room which has free-standing fireplace with low rounded belly. Recessed circular spotlights in ceiling seven feet up cast shadows of arches on wall behind fire.

Guests, who take off shoes when they enter cave with legless chairs and couches and low TV and pictures, don't stay uptight, say hosts with many interests. Art has workroom in plastered alcove; both have places to be alone.

Rhoden's metal-and-teak sculptures decorate home; his wife's paintings add character.

Bargains kept costs down; barbershop mirror cost $5; antique bricks come from demolition crews.

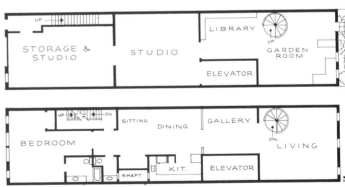

Sculptures and other art come up from basement/studio on old garage's huge elevator.

$14,000 Bought Brooklyn Garage, Now Four-Floor Home

In 1958, the gifted black sculptor John Rhoden, winner of Fulbright, Prix de Rome, and Guggenheim fellowships and a score of sculpture awards, gave a broker $200 in earnest money for a parking garage, sale-priced at $14,000 on a 25 × 112-foot city lot in a quiet middle-class section of Brooklyn. His intention: to make the big red brick building into a studio-home for him and his wife, a talented artist who has Cherokee blood. Blocked for two years by pressuring neighbors hostile to an interracial marriage and to any couple wanting to live in a building with grease pits and a car wash, the Rhodens did not become owners until 1960. Then, with their plans well formulated, they went to work.

Because Mr. Roden did the remodeling and found bargains as buildings came down, conversion cost only $3500. He put slate (discarded school blackboards) on his floors, made kitchen countertops of marble from a demolished bank, put in an iron rail banister from a firehouse, and planted trees from the Brooklyn Botanical Gardens.

The Rhodens' beautifully groomed home, from its roof garden with fountains and flowers down to its brickyard with stone sculptures and plants, is a showplace. In their neighborhood, designated a historic area by the National Park Service, their remodeled garage is appreciated by all.

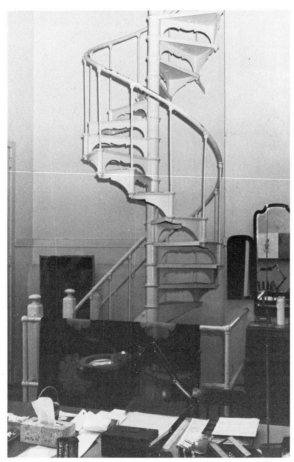

Glorious 40 × 24-foot living room, once firemen's dormitory, contains many colors, textures, cultures. Heirloom piano and chair from Philippines stand near owner's graphics under Egyptian tent turned inside down.

Twenty-six steps go down to office next to Mark Adams' 17-foot-high studio, one-time garage for fire engines. There he works in full scale on commissioned stained-glass windows and designs for vivid tapestries.

Only $7500 for Fire Station That Needed Little Done

In 1959, Mark Adams, California tapestry maker, and his wife, Beth Van Hoesen, whose intaglio prints are sold through West Coast galleries, bid $7500 for a fire station at a San Francisco auction. Their offer, the minimum acceptable to city, was high because no others could see how to use this 25 × 90-foot building on its 114-foot lot in a residential district, zoned against factories and shops. Result: two gifted people became the owners of a beautiful brick building with water, electricity, steam heat, a bathroom, handball court, and an enclosed dining room from station, left over from the days when firemen had horses and preferred to eat in a separate building.

With no more expense than the average buyer spends to do over a home for his family's needs, Mark Adams, with the help of architect friend Albert Lanier, converted the upstairs dormitory into a magnificent apartment with a gallery living room, dining area, kitchen, bedroom and study, as shown below. Then the artists concentrated on the lower level, which has had a poured concrete floor since the long-ago advent of heavy horseless trucks. They made the garage into an office and studio for Mark, an adjoining firemen's sitting room into Beth's studio, handball court into a garden, and the outdoor kitchen into a press room for printmaking. Their furnishings are as marvelously right as the layout, and many pieces were bargains as surprising as the building.

154

Heavy copper doors through which fire horses charged open today into courtyard with leafy green walls. There, clients on way to office or studios are welcomed by owners who work in ground-floor suites.

Once cream and brown, old stucco building is now brick red. Firehouse flagpole stands, but sliding pole from old dormitory to garage was cut off on advice of chief. New stairway goes up at right.

On Castro Hill in San Francisco's Mission Hill district, where buyer of public building can convert to studio but not to shop or factory, artists Mark Adams and Beth Van Hoesen got bargain of a decade at city auction. Firehouse is now their studio home.

OPPOSITE, TOP LEFT: Under canopy of parachute cloth (bought as surplus) bed overlooking garden has early American quilt, hand-embroidered pillow covers.

OPPOSITE, TOP RIGHT: Tapestry woven in France from Adams' design enriches dining area separated from kitchen by hand-cut masonite. Mexican chairs are from Cost Plus cut-rate store; top of sliding pole is at right.

OPPOSITE, BOTTOM: Space-saving kitchen without windows was approved by building inspector when skylight and ventilator went into firemen's old locker room. Tiffany lamp came from auction; counter is door covered with checked plastic; filigreed screen opens as pass-through.

ABOVE: Adams designed chair, exchanged paintings for Oriental rug, made wall cabinet for books, records, and curios like Egyptian mummy, Mexican carvings, hand-woven cheese basket, antique fishhook. He found brass lamp at junk shop, made another with soy barrel and pleated paper, mounted oak top of Navy mess table on stone blocks for coffee table, got South American fox rug for couch at half-price sale.

Beth Van Hoesen has white-walled garden with cement floor between studio and press room where she makes prints of engravings and etchings. Exotic plants in big pots prosper in California sunshine, and owners are glad they bid.

15.
Grist for the Competent Remodeler:
A Great Big Mill

Built in 1802 to withstand violent weather and vibrating millstones, this remodeled gristmill is as strong as it was when farmers carted corn, wheat, oats, and buckwheat to its loading platform. It rises tall on its granite foundation beside the Piscataquog River at New Boston, New Hampshire, beside its millpond below a dam that insured a dependable flow of water to power its grindstones. Bought in 1961 for $3500 by a twenty-two-year-old engineer, who has since married, it is now a family home. Millstones (in their vat of vertical boards) and gate-opening wheel that let water come under the building are conversation pieces.

In winter in old days, farmers from miles around came to pick up flour ground and stored by miller at harvest time.

Mill with clapboard exterior, painted red, rests on foundation dug below frost line. Loading platform is entrance; stalls for customers' horses became garage; old toilet over river is laundry.

Walls are braced frames with heavy timber posts at corners. Huge girts run from post to post and all parts are joined by mortise joints with tenons held in place with hand-hewn wooden pegs.

In May of '63, the H. Randall Parkers cleaned out the old mill Mr. Parker had bought as an investment after graduating from Cornell University and made plans to convert. Soon they had the mill set level, re-roofed with asphalt shingles, electrified (by Randy), painted outside (by a local painter) and inside (by Gail, who also scraped whitewash from beams). All rooms downstairs (living room, kitchen and dining room on platform, bedroom, study, and bath) had new windows, oak floorboards, and pine beams where needed and were furnished with gifts from family and friends. Household water came filtered from the river, and a sewage system was there.

The Parkers moved in and, as their three children came, put four bedrooms and a bath upstairs, changed downstairs bedroom to a study. Their home is one of town's largest, yet cost of remodeling (including dam repair *and furnishings*) was only $19,500.

Children can fish from door above sluiceway which was final passage through which water flowed to wheel (later replaced by turbines). Sluice gate controlled flow.

Lower level (36 × 40 feet) is mostly living room, which has 10½-foot ceiling and five 12-over-12 windows overlooking river, which is beautiful year-round and spectacular in fall.

Room is large enough to contain billiard table, 8-foot deacon's bench and 11 × 4-foot table (made from slab of King's Arrow pine) which seats twenty-six at Thanksgiving without crowding.

Because mill's operation called for grain coming down chutes to one level after another, converted home has rooms on many plateaus. Kitchen and dining area are on "stage" overlooking living room.

Step-up bedrooms are above raised kitchen. Mrs. Parker made stencils for hall, bedrooms and cupola (above) where miller checked level of stream. Entire home is conversation piece.

The one-half acre that came with Randy Parker's mill contained the millpond, the river by their house, and enough land on the downstream for a septic system. With this came rights to the dam and power. "This will give me a chance," the owner told his friends, "to generate power for our own lighting and heat someday."

In 1964, the farsighted Parkers set about repairing the log and plank dam, which was in disrepair. (Water was leaking down behind, some of the secondary supports were gone, and the top boards were rotted.) To get at their work that summer, they let water out of the pond through the old sluiceway in the cellar.

The owners knew that dams had to be built as durably as mills in the old days, when the breaking of one could mean the destruction of many mills downstream. Still, they were delighted to find the bed log (30 inches wide, 60 feet long) securely in place

after 170 years. With the help of friends, they jacked up the frame, removed rotted logs and replanked with spruce and hemlock cut at the sawmill. By fall foliage time, when many artists and photographers usually come to paint and film the millpond, the water had risen to its usual level.

The Parkers enjoy the river in the winter, when they blow the snow off the pond for skating. Later, they listen to high water and thundering ice coming over the dam as a herald to spring. In the summer, they swim and fish below the falls where the state stocks the stream with trout. And in the fall, they thrill with artists to the red, yellow, and orange trees and blue sky reflected in their pond.

Owners drink and bathe in water from the Piscataquog, pumping it from the pond into a pressure tank, where it is chlorinated and filtered. The water has a golden tint but is soft, tests "drinkable" and is cold (or anyway, cool) much of the year.

Note in the plan how the living room, dining room, and kitchen together have nine windows overlooking the river and how bedrooms above have more. A practical house, with plenty of get-away-from-everybody space for parents and each of their three children, it is an aesthetic experience for the Parkers to live by the river every day of the year. And for others who stop by anytime!

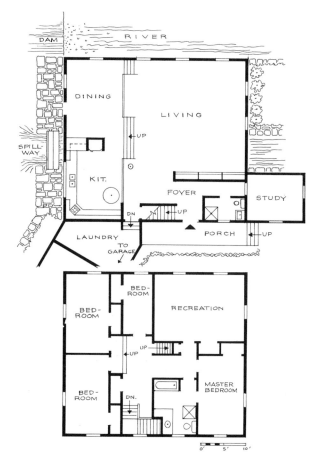

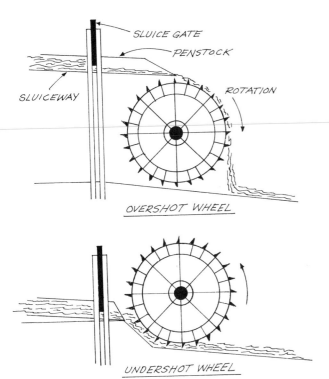

SLUICE GATE
PENSTOCK
SLUICEWAY
ROTATION

OVERSHOT WHEEL

UNDERSHOT WHEEL

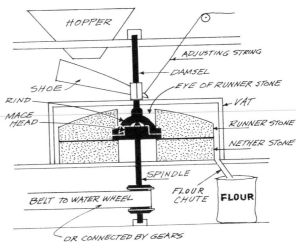

HOPPER
ADJUSTING STRING
DAMSEL
SHOE
EYE OF RUNNER STONE
RIND
VAT
MACE HEAD
RUNNER STONE
NETHER STONE
SPINDLE
BELT TO WATER WHEEL
FLOUR CHUTE
FLOUR
OR CONNECTED BY GEARS

This diagram explains how the force of water flowing against a wheel can make it turn. In early mills, attached shafts, gears and/or wheels caused a grinding stone to turn, a fulling hammer to pound cloth, or a carding machine to untangle loose wool. Not all waterpower wheels are vertical. Some were horizontal. These were modified later to become tub wheels, which led to the invention of the turbine.

The Jewel Mill

NOW A JEWEL MILL, this one-time fulling mill at Rowley, Massachusetts, went up in 1643 to clean, felt, and shrink woolen cloth that came off the loom in the English colonies. Its old water-power system is used to polish gems.

In fulling mills, a shaft connected to a water-wheel had cams at one end that raised a large wooden hammer. This pounded and turned cloth in a vat of water containing caustic animal urine or fuller's earth.

163

Pennsylvania Grist Mill
Is Home of Many Uses

In 1965, Raymond Barger, a sculptor, and his wife, Lilias, a knowledgeable antique dealer, extraordinary cook, and accomplished musician who has studied at Juilliard and at Aix-en-Provence, France, were driving through Pennsylvania. In a bend-in-the-road town they came upon an abandoned mill with a stone wall and a mansard roof which they knew instinctively was for them. Within weeks, they had bought the place for $25,000 and were hard at work doing it over as a sculptor's studio, antique shop, and home for them and their three children. Ever since, they have lived and worked in a rural retreat that is as practical for their purposes as it is romantic.

Mr. Barger's working studio and his wife's antique shop are on the first floor; five bedrooms, three baths and children's study places are on third; kitchen, dining room, sitting room, and musician's studio interconnected with open spaces are on second.

Although the building's stone shell was strong when the Bargers bought, the mill was filled with mice and its roof and floors were riddled. The Bargers cleaned the mill, stripped some of its walls down to stone, replastered others, and laid a tile floor on the second floor where they cook, dine, and entertain. Rare antiques indoors and Barger's sculptures outdoors and out make the mill a showplace.

Bucks County gristmill (also, sawmill) has white marble date stone in front wall that reads, "Built 1784—rebuilt 1894." Grain went to third floor in sack hoist attached to roof over top door.

Now an imposing country house, the mill (powered until mid-twentieth century by a 35-hp engine and the river) has more purposes than it has residents. Its gardens and expansive lawn are display area for Mr. Barger's metal monoliths that depict the progress of man and the continuing need for interaction. One half of a first floor is a studio where the sculptor works out plans and makes models for abstract forms like his three-tone copper "Transition" that stands in front of New York's J. C. Penney Building. Space across hall is Mrs. Barger's antique shop where seekers after rare Venetian, French, and Italian pieces from her round-the-world collection as well as Pennsylvania Dutch primitives are offered fresh-brewed coffee, newly steeped tea and, maybe, a fresh-baked apricot tart, marzipan torte or apple pie with Calvados. Sometimes they may be invited upstairs for a superb dinner, prepared by the hostess, after which she will play for them on her 1900 Steinway.

Stairway with copper railing circles from first to third floor. Its thirty-four treads were made by owner, who cut hole for stairwell. Spiral unifies disparate pieces, suggests harmony of family's interests.

Equality sculpture is in garden outside of Mr. Barger's studio (with skylight), formerly a shed.

A home where "everything but the children is for sale" could be commercial in feeling, but this one is not. Antiques brought from estate sales and auctions by Mrs. Barger, who attends three a week, go up to the second floor for family enjoyment before the pieces go to shop, and are often bought from this room by guests who can't wait to buy chandelier (once a church cupola) or nineteenth-century Dutch painting.

From the window on second, visitors can look down into the garden at Mr. Barger's meaningful *Equality* sculpture, with interlocked parts, which he now has copied in heavy metal as a neckpiece for guests who ask to buy. (Hung on a chain, two equal pieces mesh automatically when worn around the neck.) So popular have the sculpture and its copies become that the old mill itself is often called "equality," which the Bargers feel is fitting for a home in the heart of Mennonite country.

According to the owners, the floor of the main room is supported by 100-foot upright pine sticks in underground canal. Heating units are under Spanish tiles. One wall has been stripped of plaster down to stone, the other painted white.

Cups hang from a French bottle dryer standing on an 1850 baker's table. A plate rack from Provence is mounted near a shuttered window behind ladderback chairs around a Louis XV table. Whisks, cookie cutters, and other primitive utensils hang near planters hung from chains that were cut from a crane used for hoisting grain.

Daisies nod in a hand-painted pitcher on slab of black marble in front of hutch across from gold table from a New York mansion. Shelves hold old batter jugs and tiles.

A fantastic collection under a ceiling which has beams cut from timbers that were floated down the river from forests hundreds of miles away and sawed in mill.

Kitchen has work surfaces of slate, spices pigeonholed in post office boxes, earthenware plates.

In 1968, we paid $3,000 for Connecticut station at Gaylordsville (where James Thurber got off train in his story "The Lady on 142"). Getting approval to move building 400 yards took years.

Depot (c. 1915) had what Thurber described as "the wood, leather and smoke smell of all country railroad stations." Chestnut-beamed freight area would be living room; waiting room, a bedroom.

16.
What to Do with a Railroad Station

When we bought our station in 1968, its history, which began in 1841 when an innkeeper bought land where tracks would go north, interested us as much as conversion.

With 300 strategic Connecticut acres, the old-time Yankee told the railroad, "You can go through if your trains stop for victualing at my inn, where I'll run your ticket office." The deal lasted thirty years until trains put on diners, and even afterward, the innkeeper (and later his heirs) sold tickets. But in 1915, when the railroad was shipping much of our valley's million-dollar tobacco crop, the New Haven sent word to the inn: "We're sending up a new station master." When the proprietor shot back, "Then you'd better send up a new station," the railroad put up a station with a ticket office, waiting room, and 40-foot freight room with sliding doors.

When we saw the Gaylordsville station, we remembered the World War II spy spoof

In an 1883 history book we read of spring "which comes out near tracks a short distance below stop" where Revolutionary troops picnicked on way to Ethan Allen. For $1600, we bought hill.

by the late James Thurber, who dreamed of derring-do aboard a train from Cornwall Bridge, awakening when the conductor hollered, "*Gay-lordsville!*"

After buying, we remembered that a deacon named Gaylord once joined Revolutionary soldiers with a bottle of applejack on a hillside with a spring. We found the water, bought land there, and moved the station.

Before transporting station we were pretty sure of how we wanted our home to look. We would use 20 × 60-foot depot for upper floor, put sitting and dining room area, powder room, kitchen, and garage below. We got everything worked out on paper.

On upper floor we would have living room with balcony, two bedrooms, two baths, and study (in ticket office). Before remodeling, we would move depot to excavation and rest it on 8-foot-high poured concrete foundation walls.

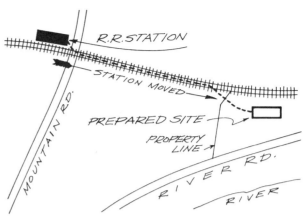

To move station south on tracks as planned we agreed to pay for $2 million insurance policy for Penn Central (new owner of railroad) for moving day, hire flagman, and repair tracks if damaged. Only then could we go, *and this was after a three-year campaign.*

The decision was to move the station (on dollies which would straddle the tracks) 400 yards down the roadbed to our new property. There we would take the building down the slope to 20 × 60-foot excavation for remodeling at a later time. All this had been studied and agreed to by an experienced house mover who would insure our building during its trip and would charge us $4000 for getting it to the new site. Once there, we would build a driveway to our newly located depot from River Road, a winding country lane at the base of our hill between the site we had selected and the Housatonic River. Later, we would bring water to the building from the spring which emerged at the base of our hill. Having thought this through, we were ready to go, as scheduled on October 9, 1971.

1. At 10 A.M. on moving day, our 60-foot station rumbled down the tracks on rubber dollies behind a 5-ton stake truck over ties laid 130 years before. By noon, it had passed the intersection and was in the woods.

2. Hauled by a cable wound on the cylinder of a winch geared to the truck, the building moved along with a minimum of jerking. Guided by experienced movers, it left tracks without mishap 400 yards from crossing.

3. Ready at bottom of prepared ramp, extending from tracks to site were cement footings laid previously. Here truck with winch moved to back of building, restraining station with ropes to avoid too rapid descent.

4. Earth ramp came down from track where there was no big drop off and no large trees. Building was held from behind by one truck as second came forward to bring station to platform made of planks on pilings.

5. Planks laid the long way across stacks of pilings formed a smooth runway over which dolly wheels could travel. Next step: temporary piers will support building; platform and dollies will be removed.

6. Mover left at this stage to return when concrete foundation has been poured and is hard. Mover will jack up building, remove piers, lower building to rest on concrete walls. Rotted siding will be replaced.

7. Cement contractor came now to put forms around base of building into which concrete for foundation will be poured. When concrete hardens and building is lowered, open space underneath will become lower floor of home.

8. By month's end, concrete had been poured, and mover was ready to return to remove piers and lower building. Before mid-November, station roof had been repaired, building was enclosed, and carpenters were busy inside.

First big job after station's move: removal and replacement of patchwork siding under wainscot trim. Tar paper went over sheathing; then clapboard. Door at right was closed off.

Garage eventually went under north side of station where cars come up driveway from road below right. Stone steps lead to entrance from parking area.

OUR PLAN when we bought the station was to convert and rent as we have remodeled and made homes for others out of a barn and cabins described earlier. But as expenses mounted, we began to see that this was impractical. (Renovation was going to be more time-consuming in this case, more complicated and costlier.) Our best bet was to rent the home we then lived in furnished, move to the station, convert, furnish, and then decide whether to stay or move back to Squash Hollow.

By November, we had a sound two-floor 20 × 60-foot box on a good piece of land for which we had paid $12,000 (for purchase, moving, foundation and repair). We could either fix this up with a minimum outlay or spend $60,000 or $70,000 on a marvelous home (with a caboose for a guest house and a swimming pool) to live in or resell. Deciding on the latter, we advertised our present home (which was mortgage-free) as a rental for the following Memorial Day, finding tenants in advance who signed a year's lease at $530 a month rent. Then, we went to the Colonial Bank and Trust for a $55,000 construction mortgage, which was approved. (At 7¾% interest, our monthly payment would be $451.53, to be taken care of by our income from the old house.)

Looking ahead to moving to the station before June 1, we hired two carpenters full time for the winter and spring months. (We did all buying of materials, planning, and supervising and helped as needed as they did interior construction. By the end of May when our renters were due, we could move into the station.

That summer, we put in a swimming pool, bought a caboose and furnished our house around us, knowing we would stay. (In another year, when our tenants moved out of our Squash Hollow house, we made it into a duplex, renting each side for $265 a month which we felt was a safer bet than to seek one renter for twice that.) By the summer of 1973, we were settled in the station.

Vertical timbers set 10 feet apart support station, which had waiting room, now bedroom (right); ticket office, now study; 40-foot freight area, now guest room and bath plus 30-foot living room with decks on two sides.

Extension provides space for larger guest room and deck above, larger kitchen and patio below. Ticket office bay window (farther left) was repaired where removed semaphore left hole and water caused rot.

The most tedious job was to make the old service floor in the freight depot right for living room. Pine planks (2 × 8 inches) had been laid down green so had shrunk, leaving gaps which had filled with mud and coal dust. Dirt had to be scraped and picked out with a screwdriver and cracks had to be filled with sized strips of wood before the floor could be sanded, stained, and waxed.

The high-ceilinged freight area which is now our upstairs living room is spacious enough for trees, several groupings of furniture, massive fireplace, and writing desk made from door. Balcony has couches.

Sculptured pot (above) was commissioned by New York hotel from potter, Al Davis, who found a crack before delivery and offered the pot at a reduced price.

The rug came from Greece, the chair from Plaza Hotel oak room, now redone; the painting of station is by Richard Schmid.

Entrance comes through door where there was a window. Stairway goes down to lower living room built into excavation. Balcony has 1 × 4-inch slats with sheet-rock panels behind them. Stairs have second fold-out flight to the depot's old attic.

The shelves at north end are 10-inch five-quarters pine boards, stained walnut to match overhead beams which tie building together.

The curios on the shelves are mementos of research projects. The Apache tray came from the reservation where we wrote a children's book; French game, from Paris where we had an advertising assignment; whale-bone mask, applehead and kachina dolls, from picture-taking sessions for a folk-art book; Winston Churchill, from a trip we made to London. Chinese rug, weathervane, coach light, and other antiques came from nearby country auctions.

174

A massive fireplace at the end of the room where there was a sliding wooden door is made with cut stones from a 75-foot retaining wall located across the tracks from the original site of the station which came with the property that we bought from the railroad. The large double window in the east wall to the right of the fireplace and sliding glass doors opposite were wooden doors when trucks came to the depot with freight. The room has effective cross ventilation and is cooled by ceiling fan, which is a replica of old-time fan, bought mail order.

At dinner parties, guests in our home are served upstairs during the cocktail hour, where on warm evenings they can walk to the deck on the right to watch the sun go down or to the deck on the left which has view of the swimming pool. Later, they go downstairs (behind twin beige chairs on left), where we also have fireplace.

With chestnut timbers standing upright every 10 feet, sectioning off station for rooms, doors and windows made remodeling easy at the planning stage. (Naturally, sliding glass windows and doors would go in between posts, partitions could extend horizontally from west post to east post, decks could match inner sectioning.) Simple to figure out upstairs as a tennis court, the living room and deck on the west side could be three 10-foot sections long, and could have on east side two-section deck (with one section left for the entrance). Extending back from living room to the bedroom could be a hall with 3-foot closet and 7-foot bathroom on east side, one 10-foot section for a bedroom on the west. Behind that could be a 10-foot study, opposite the bathroom in the el of the bedroom, to go in the space in the last 10-foot section. Outside the old waiting-room door could be another deck.

Window that looked out on tracks now gives view of river.

Old ticket office with rebuilt window (where semaphore left a hole that let in water) is now an office. Reference books line the wall at left, and files and supplies are under work table. Carpet is pale green, walls are original novelty siding painted white. Opposite the brown-trimmed window is a brown hide-a-bed couch.

Wall decorations are a print from Museum of Modern Art of Hopper's "House by the Railroad Tracks" and enlarged photograph of family aunt beside the steam train which took her west in 1911 when she was elocutionist hired by the Santa Fe to entertain railroad families. The ledge of the ticket window holds a telephone during day, a small TV set for bedroom viewing at night. The room can be a guest room in emergency, and the sofa bed downstairs can accommodate sleepers. Most guests prefer the caboose, however.

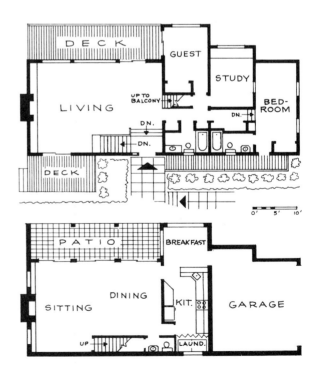

Door of bedroom opens to deck to left of swimming pool.

The hallway from the living room (once a freight area) ends at steps that go down to the bedroom, once a waiting room. (Potbelly stove that stood in middle of room and oak benches, which we could have used in caboose, were stolen between the time we offered to buy and closing.) The bathroom is built behind the closet into el at right of the dressing table; huge, fabric-covered sliding board above the left side of closet opens to a storage space built for luggage. The ticket window is next to the long mirror at right of bed; original door opens to new deck leading to a swimming pool.

The guest room down the hall on the west side of station opens to the same long deck that borders the living room. Spreads and draperies in the bedroom came from Crete; pottery lamp and vessel are Al Davis originals; Hopi basket is Arizonan.

Light carpeting, spreads in neutral shade, curtainless window overlooking Housatonic River and hills beyond give feeling of space to small guest room.

Deck where guests have morning coffee and bath across hall serve as addition to living room and powder room when large groups come for cocktails and buffet.

Dining area downstairs has custom made buffet of stained oak with brown marble top, leather chairs made originally for Plaza Hotel's Oak Room, cornucopia from Carole Stupell's Thanksgiving display.

Walnut-paneled 30-foot living and dining area with same size patio has fireplace of antique bricks, stereo, TV, books, convertible couch, curtains from Mykonos, Tiffany lamp, brass birds from Mystic, orange carpet.

In sunny extension of 10-foot-wide kitchen (below guest room), brown furnishings suggest a Greek tavern. Antique hutch table is turned long way for buffets, when guests serve themselves.

Groceries come through door from 20-foot garage to kitchen which reflects our life-style. Walnut counter separates work area from table for two, suggests aisle to dining room.

Dark wood-paneled bifold door separates General Electric laundry equipment from GE refrigerator, range with two ovens and dishwasher in Harvest Gold. Wall trim is filigreed plywood; floor tiles, dark red asbestos vinyl.

An 1899 caboose became our guest house after we sent a $400 bid to a Boston and Maine auction and ended up owner. This was not a bargain, because we found our caboose on an old Massachusetts spur where it had to be derricked to another track ($250) for shipping. We had to have its brakes repaired ($500) before it could be sent "on steel" for $200 plus to the ridge behind our stockade fence. We had to derrick it off in sections ($750) and put it back together near our pool on a short track where its wheels would not sink into the ground. So we paid close to $2000 for a caboose sold for less by companies shipping f.o.b.

Still, we are delighted with our wooden caboose (far more interesting to buffs than steel); it has four sleeping places on built-in trunks, table space, coat closet, water closet, and a cupola where train men looked for robbers, bums, and clinkers. In 1972, we re-roofed and painted the caboose and built a "station platform." We bought blue waterproof carpeting and a small TV set, range, refrigerator, and table and chairs for guests, put a chemical toilet in the old water closet and filled a huge glass bottle with water from our spring, which supplies the main house and fills the pool.

Our monolithic swimming pool, poured by Rizzo Pools of Newington, is seamless and as unpretentious and tailored-looking as the station, caboose, and plot plan. Stone steps lead into the shallow end of the water, and an agitator at the deep end gives a back massage to any swimmer who stops nearby. (There is also a heater, left unused since the energy crisis.) The water in which we swim directly from bed from May to October is sparkling clean.

More than a converted home, our made-over railroad station (with its caboose, walks, trees and flowers) is a way of life.

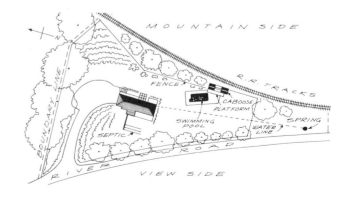

Georgia Station and Warehouse Become Elegant Entertainment Complex

Southern Railway's magnificent station in Athens, Georgia, serviced passengers from 1909 until the '30s. Waiting rooms for "ladies and gentlemen" and "colored" are integrated dining rooms.

Leased in the 1970s by youthful Lee Epting for five years with option to renew, "The Station" has private dining rooms, banquet hall, Grand Cabaret with top entertainers and The Saloon.

Walls and floors were sand-blasted to bring out old textures; furnishings are authentic; memorabilia have come from everywhere. In bar (once ticket office) window came from Harvard.

Elegant 1917 dining car, purchased for $5000 from the Tennessee Valley Railroad Museum and restored at Chattanooga, has old-time place settings. Chef was trained at Brennans in New Orleans.

Freight warehouse, where steam engines hauled in cotton on flat cars, contains nine shops, an art gallery and tavern, all different. Beer garden has rinky-tink piano, potbelly stove, Tiffany lamps.

Epting, who leases five acres and buildings on two sides of track, rents out 1200 feet of space plus balcony to owners of real estate office and antique, dress, and gift shops.

Some Remodelers Leave Station "As Is," Others Go Conventional

Lois and William Bradford, decorator and antique dealer in Sheffield, Connecticut, like their old-fashioned depot above. The Jasper Frogges of Centerville, Iowa, bought their station for its materials, then rebuilt as a conventional home (below).

The Bradfords bought for "$1000 if you take it away" from Penn Central, transported the station a few miles down the road for $2800, filled in a hole they left by the tracks ($200), put in a new foundation ($2500), and reroofed for $2500. Preserving the quaint exterior, they gave interior drama.

Jasper Frogge bought his Milwaukee station for $365 at Powersville, Missouri, dismantled it himself, and loaded and drove eleven truckloads of materials (including 8000 bricks from a railroad platform) to 80 acres he owns in Iowa. He borrowed $6000 for which he pays $37 a month on long-term FHA mortgage and made modern home.

Entryway of Bradford home with antique fixtures opens to long view of octagonal den and distant living room. Bedroom balcony with bath has railings on two sides.

Stone depot was for sale, Iowans said, but when we wrote to Chicago, Rock Island and Pacific Railway, Des Moines 50309, we heard, "No, but you can buy another station at Manly, Iowa; Simla, Colorado; or Glenville, Minnesota."

Total cost of 33 × 10-foot caboose guest house owned by Edith Stallings, former dean of women at University of Georgia, was $1500 (for purchase, moving to back yard on rolling logs, plumbing, wiring, lumber, painting.)

HOW TO BUY A RAILROAD STATION AND A CABOOSE

Sometimes you can buy an abandoned railroad station *with land*, which can be converted in its present location, but often you must buy with the idea of transporting, and for obvious reasons this is *always* true when you buy a caboose. So buy a station only if you have a site where you can convert, and buy a caboose only if you have land near a track. (A caboose weighing 39,000 pounds without wheels, which was the weight of U. of Georgia dean's caboose, can wreck the paving.)

Best way to find out how to buy a station or caboose is to write to the railroad company that serves your town. You can't dicker much when buying from a railroad, but you don't have to pay broker's commission.

Traveling through Stuart, Iowa, near Des Moines, we saw a large stone railroad station, apparently unused, which we believed could be made into four attractive apartments. When we wrote to the Rock Island Railroad, we heard that this station was not for sale, but that others were available.

To buy a caboose, write to division railroad engineer or sales agent of desired company, and ask to be notified if a caboose comes up for sale. Recently, we heard from Penn Central that bids would be accepted for two wooden cabooses, with cupola (minimum bid $1800), on one without cupola ($1000) at a coming sale, *to be delivered "as is"* to any point on Penn Central tracks. Transportation can be more costly than caboose, so be sure that delivery is included in price.

Cornwall Bridge station where James Thurber bought tickets to the station we have remodeled at Gaylordsville was recently bought from Penn Central by Dave and Marion Williams, who have now remodeled as home.

Collector's-item caboose from Colorado and Southern was parked in small town between Breckenridge and Denver. Caboose is wooden, not latter-day steel; invaluable because it was built for narrow-gauge tracks.

17.
Three Barns by Converters
Who Knew What They Were Doing

Entrance to Eric Sloane's home has chestnut timber from old barn for lamppost; split rails from old fence for railing; fieldstones, rocks and granite slab from old foundation for steps.

Eric Sloane, gifted artist, collector and author whose *Age of Barns* is a classic, lives as you hope to find him—*in a barn.*

Built on a knoll, his barn with its double-sloped gambrel roof and siding of horizontal boards, painted red, could be the reincarnation of Sloane barn paintings, internationally known. Entered at grade level on its north side, the barn has a rear door down a level. This leads to a sunny patio with a rough dry wall made of fieldstones.

Below the barn is a pond. Bulldozed out by owner, who knew that a spring (which he prefers on property to a brook) was in the valley when he bought the barn and 50 acres near Warren, Connecticut. "A brook," he says, "can dry up."

Sloane likes "working with a weather-wise box," says a barn has been made to last and is fitted to the contours of the land. "You can build as you plan and plan as you build." He has integrated his museum-type collection of early American tools, carvings, and furniture with the architecture itself.

Kitchen work table was carpenter's bench; planter was washstand; ceramic tiles with birds and flowers are Sloane originals. Old bricks for floor are glazed; antique bells are peace symbols.

Head of John Adams on slaughtering table is opposite church pew next to couch made from logging sled. Carpenter suggested window overlooking pond where artist first planned fireplace.

Early American chessboards hang above chestnut mantel on brick fireplace opposite window above pond. Hourglass collection is at right of sawed table. Lamp bases are clock and barbershop pole.

Unforgettable room is 25 × 36 feet with 10-foot ceilings. Floorboards (25 inches wide) were cut in local mill. Paintings on wall are Sloane's, which he usually frames with barn siding.

Dough trough is coffee table; wall decorations are bedwarmers and tavern and bootshop signs; pillow covers are needlepoint; some rugs are hooked, others are shag. Beams are from Nova Scotia.

Barbershop pole is newel post for stairway with boat's oar for railing. Wrought-iron door handle, hooked rug with eagle, and pewter mug and iron bank on mantel are from bygone era.

Red brick water tower (c. 1905) supplied water to 300-acre Princeton estate, included cavernous wagon rooms, workers' rooms, and sheepfold. Like Kelleher barn, it's treated differently.

Owners tore down wall and enclosed shelter for glassed-in dining room overlooking old sheep yard, made two odd-shaped "nooks" into impeccable sitting room and get-away study.

Artist's abstract painting over fireplace is focal point in stark, gleaming 30 × 50-foot living room. Uncluttered grouping of chairs and couches includes owner-designed cube-shaped cabinets.

Artist's Home Contains Duplex Studio

As dramatic as the Kelleher home in Princeton (but not as dramatic a bargain because the owner is the second remodeler), this converted sheepfold was built originally at Drumthwacket. Now the Tudor-style building is a working studio for painter and printmaker Thomas George and home for his family.

Most memorable room is the gallery-sized living room (above) with wide-board pine flooring, scarred from sheep hoofs and rakes, but gleaming like a dance floor. The most workmanlike rooms are the artist's print room and his wife's sleek kitchen on the lower level of the tower. The most intriguing room is a "mad scientist's" hideaway in the tower filled with inventions of young Geoffrey, grandson of the late Rube Goldberg.

In converted horse barn behind immense living room, Thomas George has two-story studio with print room upstairs. Here he creates watercolors and woodcuts sold in New York and Europe.

You walk between carousel horses to enter the handsome home of Mrs. Howell, widowed Georgia grandmother who converted this dairy barn on her family's old farm.

Barn door is filled in with paned glass, above which is a glittering fanlight brought to farm from family's town house many years back by Mrs. Howell's father. "Before" picture is below.

World Traveler Goes Home to Barn

A woman of superb taste who commuted as a child from her family's town house in Atlanta to the farm where she now lives, Mrs. Max Don Howell has traveled to all parts of the world and has brought back exquisite pieces of furniture from many countries. Living in Atlanta as a widow, she had some of her collection in storage until her apartment was sold and she returned to the farm. There, next to her daughter and her daughter's family, she has converted a cowbarn, adding a new bedroom and bath in a wing at the side. She has also made a milk house into a guesthouse where she has space to display her carefully selected furnishings as they have never been presented before.

Slender, curving stairway in room with off-white walls and contrasting dark beams came from Spain. Antique mantel is handsomely carved; imported chandelier is cathedral-sized.

Soft green Aubusson rug, paired yellow bergeres and blue easy chairs are sensual delight. Marble-topped table has Chippendale legs from old sofa. Portraits over fireplace are of grandparents.

Memorable as the merry-go-round horses out front on Mrs. Howell's pierced brick wall are the painted Venetian cupboard in the corner of the living room that serves as a bar and the magnificently carved stairway that leads up to a loft made into a game room with lounge chairs, bridge table, books on shelves.

Living close to her grandchildren in one of the handsomest homes in Georgia on a farm that has been in her family for 80 years, Mrs. Howell is understandably happy in her barn. She entertains often in her milk house, which has its original rough brick wall, raw-wood ceiling, and floor of flagstones which are painted white, and covered with calfskin rugs. Only a dozen miles from Atlanta, she can get to the city whenever she wants, and she also has a home at Sea Island.

HOW TO FIND AND CONVERT A BARN

Barns are everywhere, even in towns. Not all are bargains, however, and conversion costs can be astronomical. So buy and convert with care. Look for your barn in counties where small farms are going out of business. When you see a building that you can do over, talk to its owner.

As a beginning converter, buy a small barn as a starter and later buy a barn that you can dismantle and bring to your property as an addition. Or convert only a portion of a large barn to begin with. If the barn is on slope, put the entrance on the road side with large windows and patio at lower ground level at back. Work from a plan, or build as Eric Sloane has done, making rooms in your "weather-wise box" as needed.

LEGAL ANNOUNCEMENTS

SCHOOL BLEACHERS

Notice is hereby given that sealed bids will be received by Board of Education of Union High School System District, No. 210 for the following:

From Central High School—Bid Call No. 210 for Folding Gymnasium Bleachers. Bids are to be filed with the Bus. Mgr., 415 East Grant Street, on or before 10 a.m. Thursday, and will be publicly announced in Conference Room No. 227 by the Bus. Mgr. or his authorized representative.

FARM AND OUTBUILDINGS

The Probate Court of Litchfield County hereby announces an auction of a farm and outbuildings to settle an estate with eleven heirs—(Stuart and M. E. Anderson, John and Dorothy Stout, E. J. and Dina Anastasio, Thomas and Susan Fisher, Jay, Elizabeth and Christopher Fisher)—on Friday at 2 P.M. on Bullmuck Stream, Route 7. Property consists of house, barn, shed, summer kitchen and 50 acres bisected by country road. Auctioneer to be former judge of Probate Court—Minimum bid, $12,000.

PUBLIC NOTICES

GOVERNMENT LAND

For sale by BLM Land Office, Eighth Floor, Federal Building, 125 South State Street, P.O. Box 11505, Salt Lake City, Utah 84111—Friday, 2 P.M.—by sealed bid —40 acres in SW corner bisected by steep canyon wall; part on rough canyon rim, part in canyon bottom. Irrigation ditch and town pipeline cross tract; no utilities; paved county road on tract. App. $900. (plus publication fee for four insertions) Send certified check, P.O. money order or bank draft or cashier's checks payable to Bureau of Land Management for full amount of bid which will be returned if not high. For further information, write or call BLM.

DEPOSITORY SALE BY PUBLIC BID, APRIL 2

Six rooms, 2 lavatories, lunch counter, shed consisting of 2,432 square feet under roof of wood, frame construction, to be moved, as is, from school site. Key for inspection and bid forms from District Administration Office. Sealed bids must be submitted before April 2, to DA office.

CORRECTIONAL BUILDING AND 40 ACRES

To be sold by General Services Agency, Washington, D.C.: 40 acres on water with brick garage that belonged to Federal Correctional Institution by sealed bid on Oct. 9. Send to above agency (zip code 20405) for free copy of *Buying Government Surplus Property.*

BARGAIN BUILDINGS

100-YEAR-OLD ACADEMY

Rugged century-old New England Academy building has over 2000 finished square feet. Water and electricity available, non-functional johns, slate roof, original weather-vane, 20 min. Burlington, via interstate and 10 min. to Bolton Valley. ___gst Realty, Wilton.

COMMERCIAL ICE HOUS_ ON NICOLLET ISLAND

Beautiful island in the land of the sky blue waters can be converted to magnificent home by buyer who appreciates history, natural beauty and can work with hands. Owner of old-time Minnesota ice house will hold mortgage.

OLD STAGECOACH STOP

Long before railroads, this old adobe building with beams held together with whittled pegs was southwest landmark. Can be beautiful place for family that appreciates folklore and great climate.

CHURCH TO BE CONVERTED NEAR ARTISTS' COLONY, TAOS

In long ago church built by missionaries with help of Indians, you can make new life. Building has seen many winters and is still sturdy. Romantic past, great future—Box 10—but hurry, this will go.

VICTORIAN GREENHOUSE PHILADELPHIA SUBURB

Bask in a sunny world of orange trees and camelias when the snow flies. Convert this marvelous old greenhouse for year-round living, using glassed in section for sitting and dining area. You can even have a fireplace. Will sell with plans.

OLD STORE AND WAREHOUSE ON WATER IN MANCHESTER

What others have done here on the water you can do too, with architectural help provided if needed. Make apartments in one building, convert other for you—or get income from both. Beautiful sites.

OLD OPERA HOUSE WHERE LILLIAN RUSSELL WAS STAR

Some call it a white elephant, but anyone who visited this South Carolina landmark will see possibilities for a great home. Living room can have raised section which was stage where Edwin Booth, Lillian Russell and even Sarah Bernhardt performed. Sell.

HANGOUT OF ROBERT SERVICE

Fairbanks: Fantastic old building with bar where some say Robert Service got idea for "The Shooting of Dan McGrew." No matter, bar, converted to apartments, in boom area can put gold in your pockets.

VICTORIAN WHITE ELEPHANT LOOKS LIKE STAGE SETTING FOR TENNESSEE WILLIAMS PLAY

Relic of bygone days in New Orleans, this old wreck was overlooked for years until it appeared as "steamboat gothic" joke in state magazine. Now everybody calls but timid back away. Low price to courageous buyer who will convert as historians approve.

RANGER'S CABIN IN MONTANA

Quarter section bought years ago at BLM auction has old ranger's cabin at foot of purple mountain that can be great retreat __day Zane Grey. Write McSweyn, ___ Montana 59072.

CABOOSE FOR S__ PENN CENTRAL COMPANY

Write Purchases and Material, Penn ___tral, Philadelphia, Pennsylvania 1910_ ask to be put on list for next offer o_ ___boose to be delivered on Penn ___ tracks. When you bid, certified chec_ go five days after award before deli__

RAILROAD STATION FOREST CITY, IOWA

For full information write about ___ old building to Chicago, Rock __ Pacific Railroad Co., 4th & V__ Des Moines, Iowa 50309. Also __ other stations for sale at __ Klemme, Iowa, and more in C__

BLACKSMITH'S SHOP ROCKLAND COUNTY, N.Y.

Once a repair shop for h_ blacksmith's shop can be a __ for a home. Located in res__ cannot be commercial—bu__ weekend place for a do-it-___

POSSIBILITIES UNLIMIT_ IN LITCHFIELD COUNT_

Abandoned nursery wi__ back from road can be __ sturdy factory with el__ toilets, and cabin in v__ option to buy—All are __ the air is good to brea__

COAST GUARD LIFE_ LAKE MICHIGAN

Partially restored s__ ___taurant and worked __ money—Call 312-20__

SILO AT CHEWE_

Perfect vacatio__ imagination; stu__ animals near; __ three-floor home __ mer season ho__

OWN A SHAR_

Old wharf __ can be home__ prising conve__ dominiums a__

OLD GRIST_

Live fre__ moni (wh__ lege stude__ you can __ Get tax __ Omnibu__

FORME_

Old, __ Massa__ Worl__ buye__ that __ nig__

PART THREE

HOW TO SAVE
AS YOU BUY,
CONVERT, AND FURNISH

1.
Train Yourself to See
What Others Miss

You may be passing a bargain building every day that you could convert. The trick is to see what others miss. This is an ability that you will acquire as you look at homes that others have made from something offbeat.

For years, thousands passed the old power house (opposite) which serviced the once prosperous Monument Mills at Housatonic, Massachusetts, where workers made cotton bedspreads and other textile products until the 1940s. Many who drove along the Housatonic River on Route 183 toward Glendale admired the great stone building and some even stopped to picnic there. Surprisingly, even though the power house was empty, no one asked to buy. Yet purchase would not have been difficult, because back taxes were owed on 12 acres along the water and on the building, and the town wanted to collect.

Eventually, the town took over the property, and now has decided not to sell either the house or the land, planning to use both for recreational purposes. Today, townspeople appreciate the old place on the water, where their forefathers cleared away trees and woods, built stone fences a hundred years ago so that sheep could graze near the new woolen mill. (Later, cotton was processed, too.) Other towns with similar histories also have empty buildings on which back taxes are owed. Not many want to take over such buildings, and where this is so, you may get a good buy.

Any town with a giant mill or other industry, now closed, is a great place to find a bargain. With workers gone, old halls, stores, churches, schools, inns and shops are

In New England towns, where old mills have shut down, empty buildings (churches, stores, opera house, railroad station, etc.) are often bargains.

unused. Some are held for back taxes. In such towns, ask about abandoned buildings at the assessor's office in the town hall.

"Who wants to live in a dead town?" you may be saying to yourself. But do not worry that you will have nothing to do. Most of these towns are on rivers or lakes in mountain areas, and some are close to large Eastern cities.

Don't be afraid to be first, wherever you are. When you convert a building in an unusual way, others will see. Newcomers will come to do the same, as many followed the example of Bob Griggs in Inman Park, Atlanta, and as many migrated to western ghost towns after a few farsighted residents made over saloons, stagecoach stops, jails.

No building need be too large or small. (If large, live in only part of the building until you decide what you want to do with what's left. If too small, add on.) That main point is to recognize worth in what others miss, and to buy for little so that you will have funds left to do the place over. Specific ways to save will be spelled out in this section.

This nineteenth-century stone mansion at Stone City, Iowa, was headquarters for an artists' colony directed by Grant Wood in the 1930s. Vacant for years, the home burned in the '50s, but outbuildings remain.

Having seen what others have done with silos, lighthouses, and lookout towers, you can see that the tower at the right can be a beautiful home. Yet it was overlooked as a possible living place for years, because it stands close to a great stone house built in the 1800s that has been gutted by fire. Anyone who walked up the hill to where a wealthy quarry master once lived said "What a pity," and walked away. Now, many are going up this hill, which is in Stone City, Iowa, to see where Grant Wood had his art colony in the 1930s.

Belonging to the Nissen brothers of Cedar Rapids, inventors of the trampoline, whose father rented the property to the Iowa artist during the depression, the place attracted little attention until neighbors created an annual "Stone City Festival." Now visitors from afar are going to see where Wood was born, painted his famous "Stone City" painting, and is buried. And many are looking at the old house *and tower*. What could possibly have been bought for little is now off the market. Suggestion: look behind a derelict mansion for attractive outbuildings, especially if the home has historical significance.

With privacy fence in the front, this well-groomed New Hampshire garage can be pleasant home. You don't become enthusiastic, however, until you learn this was once an ice house and backs up to beautiful millstream.

Build deck over water with approaches from lawn and through sliding glass doors at back. Keep in mind that many garages and barns are built close to road. *Always walk around building to see what's behind.*

Riding along Route 25 in Connecticut, we stopped at barn which could have nice rear view, we believed. Later, we took picture at right, which could have been taken miles from busy highway we had just left. A *find*!

Pond near house looks across to barn which can become magnificent country home. Again, we include pictures of the front and back of the barn to encourage you to look at all sides of building before saying no.

Weathered barn on stone foundation is sturdy but too close to road to orient this way. Too bad if you don't stop, because Aspetuck River is at back. Oriented to rushing stream, this chestnut barn could be glorious.

Look at barn from across river and you realize it has romantic world of its own. To train yourself to see what others miss, learn to anticipate what *might* be at other side of building. Take the time to look.

This old store on Route 7 between New Milford and Gaylordsville, Connecticut, bore a "For Sale" sign for months, but no one bothered to stop. "Who would want to run a store," a few said, "in a wreck of a place like that?"

Less than a quarter mile from the store is this magnificent abandoned quarry with white limestone walls and perfectly clear spring water of Mediterranean blue. Move the store, as shown, as start for stunning home.

Training your eye to see always involves training your mind to see. Having studied the conversions of others, you probably look twice now at freak places like this store. It will be a bargain and it can be a house, but it needs the right setting. A quarter mile away you find your site at a quarry.

This particular building is not tall so can go under wires, is narrow enough to be taken down the highway and was built in two sections so can be moved in two trips. Should the mover see a problem, you can take building apart and reassemble. With deck over water, home will be a beauty.

In the spring of 1973, this lovely Dutch house with wood frame, stucco siding, and 2432 square feet under novelty roof was offered for sale by office of school district near Phoenix.

"Who wouldn't snap this up?" Catch was that house was on slab with no sills and condition was that it had to be removed. Buyer trying to move would have nothing left but random lumber.

To move or not to move is something to consider when you see an old building offered at a low price "if you take it away." And it is something to think about when you see a lovely home in a tenement district. Study carefully, but don't jump to buy.

Sometimes even the finest building isn't worth moving.

Here are seven questions to ask yourself as you consider whether a bargain building you have to move is worth the trouble:

- Is there a site nearby that will make moving worthwhile?
- Does the building fit the site?
- Is the building on sills so that it can be transported *whole* on truck or dollies?
- Are there bridges, steep hills, railroad tracks, or overhead wires between present site and new site that will make for expense and red tape?
- If the building can't be moved whole, can you dismantle and reassemble?
- If you dismantle on your own for materials, only, will the work be worth your time?
- Moving either makes sense or isn't practical. With these guidelines, you can decide.

Roof is shot and sideboards sag, but old barn is worth dismantling for its chestnut siding, pegged timbers and rafters. Barn can be reassembled or boards and beams can be used in other conversion.

Tobacco which supported builder of barn is gone, but gravel brings dollars to owner who has mined around and inside building. Weathered boards are gone but timbers are worth moving.

Don't let bygones be bygones if you want a place that is bound to go up in value. Find a building with a meaningful past, and you have an investment in folk art. Keep nostalgia in mind, and you will sell well next year or twenty years from now. Also, your life will expand as you live with history.

When considering a building to be converted think about its past. Talk to older residents about how the building was used; find old pictures and stories at the library; talk to your historical society.

As you convert, save this history, preserve novelty siding and the ticket window in a railroad station, the grinding wheels in a mill, lifting wheel in a cotton warehouse. Without going quaint, decorate with leftovers from yesterday as conversation pieces.

Beside Housatonic River in small Massachusetts town where old-time trolley ran right up the middle of the stream, this great brick carbarn is reminder of past. It is storage place now.

Under the spreading branches, the village smithy stands no more, but his forge in many rural communties is now a home. This one on Old Forge Road, Gaylordsville, Connecticut, is owned by Historical Society.

The huge glassed porch of Heights Hotel at McGregor, Iowa (page 115), has obvious possibilities. And the new owners, John Culver (who was the youngest member of Congress when he went to Washington) and his wife, Anne, are making the most of it. They enjoy the view of the Mississippi from this porch, now their living room, which they have decorated with river scene from Mark Twain's time.

This old railroad station below stood idle for years at New Boston, New Hampshire, where it is now owned by a post of the American Legion. A handsome meeting place, it is the envy of home-seekers from Boston and New York. Happily, there are available railroad stations, just as charming and well built. So write to sales agent for whatever line is near.

In the early 1960s, a Connecticut bank settled the estate of Richard Pomeroy (who owned a mountain in a northwest county which he sold off in parcels to buyers like Mr. Blanding who built his dream house on a hill). During settlement, Aaron and Jean Seltzer of Long Island bought the farm office and a row of barns for $2500, explaining to skeptical friends, "We're going to live here weekends."

The Seltzers moved into the three-office suite which had heat, plumbing, and electricity. Soon, they put a double gate at the top and bottom of their driveway, making their many barns into a dramatically different compound. Buying from country auctions, they furnished box-shaped rooms as designers decorate showrooms. They learned much about American antiques, and in 1972 sold their city business and moved to Connecticut where they operate "Aaron's Antiques" on Route 7.

Entrance to old office on huge Pomeroy farm where owner had several houses, raised stock, and sold lumber is painted but really not changed.

Long row of barns where lumber was stored has become private living complex for couple who changed way of life when they made "purchase of a lifetime." Gates are now at two ends of drive.

Treating giant barns like a little girl's doll house, new owners cleaned, furnished, and decorated one enclosed space after another until huge home was finished. Seltzers dare you to find another home like it!

Back in the 1920s, this huge stone barn, like the one restored by Frank Morss (page 2), was a cowbarn on Iron Bank Farm near Music Mountain in Falls Village, Connecticut. On the first level, which has a cement floor, there were stanchions; above was a gymnasium-sized haymow; at the far end were living quarters for workers. In the 1960s, the barn with a few acres of land was purchased for $17,000 by a New York television announcer who made a home for his wife and children in the old workers' quarters and dreamed of turning the great open rooms in the barn into a TV production studio and Little Theater.

The announcer became ill and did not realize his dream of owning a TV production house in the country, but he did exercise an option which had been his since purchase to buy more acres. When he sold at a profit, a newcomer bought the barn, moving into the producer's apartment which had been beautifully remodeled.

Today, the two great rooms, that look like basketball courts, can still be a studio. Or they can be the genesis for a home like the Kellehers (page 30) or like the George home (page 189). In such a stone barn with vast rooms, you can do what you want. So don't worry about space. Dream a little!

CHECK LIST OF TERMS IF YOU BUY DIRECT

Definitions and what to do each step of the way.

ACRE—Measure of land approximately the size of football field—160 square rods (4,840 square yards; 43,560 square feet).
Know what acreage comes with building.

SURVEY—Determination of boundaries of tract of land.
Ask for survey map or up-to-date examination for which seller pays.

ASSESSED VALUATION—Assessment of real estate by government office for tax purposes.
At assessor's office find out (1) what percentage of market value is base for appraisal; (2) town's appraisal of property you want.

MARKET VALUE—The highest price a buyer will pay or the lowest price for which a seller will sell.
Before asking to buy, find out present market value as estimated by town from assessor or, if you prefer, from objective appraiser whom you can pay to come from bank. (Such an appraisal comes automatically when you apply for mortgage.)

MIL—One tenth of a cen; the measure used to state the tax rate. (One mil on the dollar is the same as 1/10 of 1 percent of the assessed value of the property.)
Find mil rate for tax determination at tax office.

EASEMENT—A right-of-way given to outsider through land of another.
If you need road through seller's property to get to yours, spell this out in agreement of sale and deed; if someone has right to go through what you are buying, get this cleared up before signing.

AGREEMENT OF SALE—Written agreement between you and the seller.
Clearly spell out terms of sale so that you and seller know and agree on all phases of sale in advance. (Or ask seller to have his attorney draw up a formal Contract of Sale, which your attorney can examine before you and seller sign.)

EARNEST MONEY—Your first payment (usually 10 percent of offer) as evidence of good faith.
Give to seller with Agreement of Sale, noting that money will be returned if seller does not deliver as spelled out in Agreement or you cannot get mortgage or financing as you and seller have agreed.

ESCROW—Deed or money held by third person (usually a real estate broker or banker or attorney) until sale is consummated.
In dealing without broker, ask bank or an agreed-upon attorney where you are applying for mortgage to hold money you put down.

MORTGAGE—A transfer of property to bank as security for loan you will get to pay seller.
Apply at local bank, which will send out appraiser to determine bank's risk.

BANK APPRAISAL—An objective estimate of value of property, made by bank's appraiser at no cost to you when you apply for mortgage to determine whether property is worth what bank is lending in case you default.
Look at transaction through appraiser's eyes. What will bank look for to determine what return will come from property should you be unable to pay?

EQUITY—The value owner has in property over and above mortgage against it.
Consider taking over owner's mortgage on building at low interest rate, if possible, or buying with long-time contract from owner rather than from bank if you can get lower interest rate there than at bank.

AMORTIZATION—Liquidation of debt on installment plan.
Determine with lender (bank or owner) what interest you will pay with principal and for how long you will pay.

LIEN—A hold or claim on property held by another as security for debt, judgment, mortgage, or taxes.
Make sure that any claim on property you buy has been discharged before you buy. Make this a condition in your Agreement of Sale.

ABSTRACT OF TITLE—A condensed history of the title, consisting of names of various owners plus a statement of all liens, charges or encumbrances.
You will pay an attorney to search title when you borrow. (If title is not clear, seller must remove cloud, as spelled out in your Agreement. Your aim: to end up with a marketable title, free from clouds.)

CLOSING—A session at which deed held by seller's attorney is transferred to buyer, and an accounting of funds is made to both parties. (If you are asking for mortgage, you will have closing at bank and have your own attorney and attorney of seller at the meeting.)
You will pay all bills at meeting—and go away as new title is in your name which you and/or your attorney will register.

DEED—A document by which property is transferred when signed, sealed, and delivered by seller. (Your aim: a warranty deed, which contains statement by seller that he will protect you against any claimant. However, you can settle for quitclaim deed, especially if seller holds contract, which states clearly that seller gives up all claim on property.)
Keep this in a safety deposit or strong box.

TITLE—Legal evidence of ownership.
Register this in your name at town hall or county courthouse following your closing.

2.
How to Buy the Place You Want for the Lowest Possible Cost

Here are seven rules for getting your building for the lowest possible cost:

1. Determine before calling on the owner possible reasons why he or she might sell.

If an owner has recently died, heirs will be glad to exchange a building for dollars, which are easier to divide than real estate.

Any empty building on which an owner is paying taxes while it brings in no income is a money-loser *unless the building or the land under it is appreciating in value.* Your purchase may be "found money" for owner who may not have considered that anyone would convert. Try to learn whether any previous offer has come in. (Is town considering buying old post office for day-care center? Is railroad station being considered for museum? Does carpenter want old hotel for storage space?)

Will your offer be godsend for owner in trouble? If owner is going to nursing home, her barn by river is something she doesn't even want to think about. When you ask to buy, she may accept immediately.

2. Decide before seeing owner whether top price you will pay makes sense.

Check deeds at town hall (or wherever filed) to see what former owners paid. To determine selling price on any transaction before 1968, when federal tax on real estate was repealed, count the tax stamps on a deed. (Each $1.10 in stamps stands for $1000 of the selling price, so with $11 in stamps on deed, for example, you know price was $10,000.) To determine sale price after 1968, count conveyance stamps, which in most towns are affixed at same rate. Also, check stamps on nearby parcels.

3. Train yourself to see with a bank appraiser's eye.

You can't hire an appraiser to give you an objective opinion without letting the owner know what you're up to, so study the property before making an offer, as your bank might do.

4. When you contact owner, look at yourself through his or her eyes.

If you want owner to hold mortgage note or contract, be prepared to present your credentials as you would to a banker. Have answers ready for these questions:

- How will you use the property? Owner will wonder how you will convert an outbuilding near his home.
- How will this owner enjoy living next door to you?
- Will your offer make the owner a profit worth bothering about? If owner accepts, will he be in better shape than before you called?
- How much interest will you pay? Offer to pay more interest than owner can earn from a savings account.
- How much will you pay down if he holds the mortgage contract?
  The higher your down payment the more assurance the owner has that (a) you won't default on payments, making foreclosure necessary (which is costly and a nuisance); (b) you won't be handing back a partially remodeled building; (c) he will still come out even if you renege.
- If he prefers not to hold mortgage contract, will you mortgage through a bank? This way, he can get full payment now which he may prefer.

5. When you meet with owner, don't run down his building.

You downgrade a property owner's taste when you knock his property, and your negativism shows as a bargaining tool. Tell the owner you like his building, but be sure he knows that you won't overpay.

6. Offer something in addition to money when you talk.

Offer to make floor plan for a second building that the owner may want to convert or sell. Or offer to write ad that will bring additional customers in exchange for a break on price. Show how your remodeling will help others to see what can be done.

Will owner block himself from back acres if he sells you the land you want? Offer to give owner a right-of-way. Or, if you want to buy his pond, tell him that you will allow fishing and swimming privileges. As you negotiate, keep owner's needs in mind.

7. When you make an offer that is as high as you know you should go, bid no higher, no matter how much you like the place.

Decide early what your ceiling will be. When you make this offer, explain that this is your final offer, *and walk away.* You may get a call that the property is yours. If so, fine, but in the meantime begin looking at other buildings. (Now that you can recognize possibilities that others miss, you will find another building that is right.) Soon, you will find an ideal piece of property at a price in line with what you can pay.

The suggestions above are based on the premise that you will buy direct from owner. There are two reasons for doing this. (a) You can usually get a better price from a seller who does not have to pay a broker's commission; (b) when doing your own sleuthing, you probably will find a building that is not listed with a broker. Occasionally, however, you may find yourself dealing through a real estate agent, who has either advertised a building you may be interested in or is handling a property you have stopped to see.

Here are five rules that will help you to get a reasonable price when working through a broker:

1. Treat your broker as a partner.

Your interests are this broker's interest, so expect help on what you want to accomplish, but play fair. *Never ask your broker to cut his or her commission, which is paid by the seller.* Do make suggestions that will speed up the sale.

2. Know what your broker is entitled to get from sale, but don't talk about his take.

Your local real estate board will tell you whether a broker gets 5, 6 percent or more from sale of a building, 8, 10 percent or more from sale of land. Does board have multiple listing? Then, assigned and selling brokers divide commission and board gets small percentage.

3. Play square with your broker and your broker will play square with you.

Let your broker alert other brokers to your needs, splitting the commission as desired. But don't take up one broker's time and, then, on a whim answer another's ad for property in the same area. Ask the broker with you to answer the ad.

4. Do all your business through your broker, once you accept his services.

Don't talk figures to the owner direct. Test your suggestions on your broker, who knows the seller and the community. Let your broker pass along any offer or trade.

5. Let your broker introduce you to a lawyer, bank, abstract office, surveyor, insurance man, and even carpenters, electricians, plumber, etc. This way, the broker earns the good will of others, and you become acquainted with local business people whose services will be necessary.

Keep these points in mind and, then, proceed with your broker in the same way that you would buy direct. *Keep in mind the top price over which you will not go.* Let the broker make this offer, and then walk away. Keep on the lookout for something in your price range, and you will find a place.

A small clean barn with entrances on two levels is easy to convert and is as good a buy as you can get in most rural sections. Still, you may have a problem helping a banker to see what you want to do when he has been lending money for conventional homes, not barn conversions. So think through your overall plan before you go for a loan. Then, you can talk in specifics, and you can see better how you want to do over the building.

First step, even before you work out your conversion plan is to draw up a plot plan. Assume, for example, that you have bought a small classic barn on 1½ acres on a slope near a stream. As you look at your property, decide where you will have your well, and then, with your town's sanitation rulings in mind, figure where to put your septic system. Obviously, your construction plan for kitchen and bathrooms will be affected by both, as the overall layout of your home will be affected by other plot considerations.

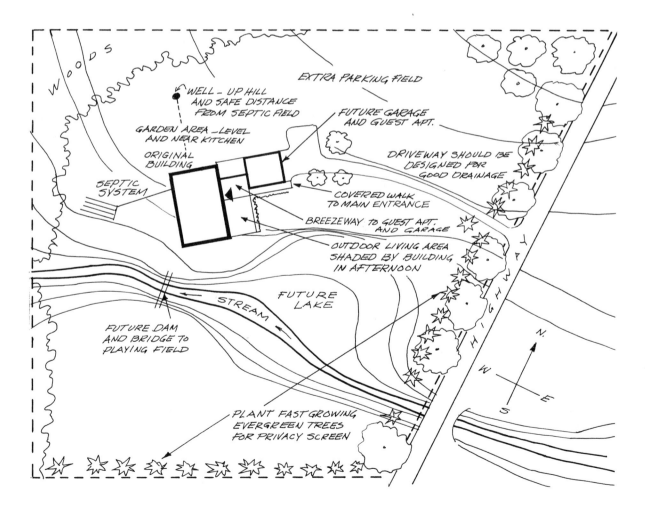

3.
Before You Build or Borrow, Think Through Your Overall Plan

Suppose you have paid $6000 in cash for a barn on 1½ acres. Rather than borrowing piecemeal to convert, work out a plot plan that may be long-range but is ideal. Decide what you want to do first, second, and third.

Draw your plot plan with your boundaries in mind (as plan opposite is drawn within boundaries of highway, stream, woods, and field). Draw a square for barn, and on hill behind make a dot for drilled well far above septic system (to right of stream in drawing and above swimming place). Call a well driller for his opinion and find out from the sanitation department how far the well must be from septic system (75 feet is our town's rule). Ask how leaching fields should relate to stream.

Talk with your Extension Service about what, when, and how to plant. Get a tube to send soil sample to the College of Agriculture for a free analysis.

Find out how to treat your land to support wildlife, clear brush, put in wind protection plantings and road screens and dam stream. If needed, *ask for technical assistance (free).*

Your overall plan will influence construction. Note how barn's plan below has kitchen and bath back-to-back on upper level, living room area at front, master bedroom with walkout to swimming.

Pay an architectural student to draw your plans for barn to scale; take the plot plan to bank for construction loan.

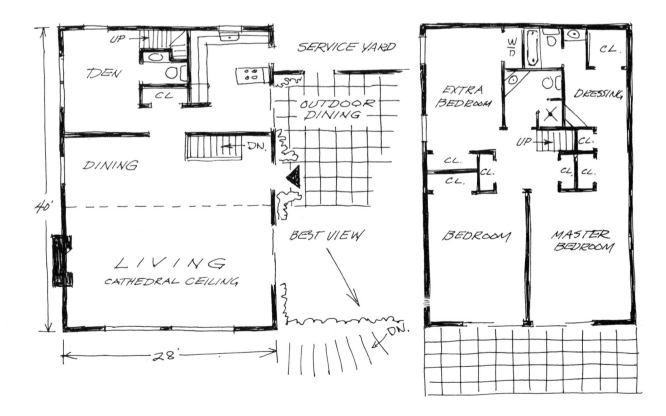

RESIDENTIAL APPRAISAL REPORT

NAME

ADDRESS

LAND DESCRIPTION

HOUSE DIMENSIONS

_____ x _____ = _____ SQ. FT.   FLOOR

_____ x _____ = _____ SQ. FT.   FLOOR

_____ x _____ = _____ SQ. FT.   FLOOR

_____ x _____ = _____ SQ. FT. BASM'T. LIVING AREA

GARAGE

_____ x _____ = _____ SQ. FT.

PORCH

_____ x _____ = _____ SQ. FT.

OTHER

_____ x _____ = _____ SQ. FT.

BUILDING STYLE		YEAR BUILT		YEAR REMODELED	

	BSM'T.	1ST FLR.	2ND FLR.	3RD.FLR.	TOTAL
BEDROOMS					
BATHS					
TOTAL ROOMS					

1ST 3RD FLRS. _____ SQ. FT.   PORCHES _____ SQ. FT.

FINISHED BASMEN'T. _____ SQ. FT.   GARAGE (NON-BSMENT) _____ SQ. FT.

(TO BE COVERED LATER BY PICTURES OF HOUSE AND STREET SCENE)

KITCHEN:

	EXCEL.	GOOD	FAIR	POOR
☐ MODERN ☐ SEMI-MODERN ☐ OLD				
BUILT-INS: ☐ CABINETS ☐ STOVE				
☐ REFRIG. ☐ DISHWASHER ☐ DISPOSAL				
☐ EXHAUST FAN ☐ FILTER HOOD				

FIREPLACES: NO. _____

WALLS ☐ SHEETROCK ☐ MARLITE / ☐ PLASTER ☐ PANELING

CEILINGS: ☐ SHEETROCK ☐ HOMOSOTE / ☐ PLASTER ☐ ACC. TILE

AMOUNT OF CLOSETS:

BATHS: WALLS ☐ CERAMIC ☐ PLASTIC ☐ MARLITE ☐ SHEETROCK ☐ VINYL ☐ MODERN ☐ SEMI-MOD ☐ OLD

FLOOR ☐ CERAMIC ☐ VINYL ☐ CARPET

FLOORS: ☐ OAK ☐ PLANK ☐ PINE ☐ LINOLEUM CARPET ON ☐ OAK ☐ PLYWOOD

DOMESTIC HOTWATER: ☐ ELECTRIC ☐ GAS ☐ OIL ☐ OFF FURNACE ☐ RENTAL CAPACITY

FOUNDATION: ☐ CONC. BLOCK ☐ STONE ☐ CONCRETE ☐ CINDER BLOCK

BASEMENT: _____ % FULL _____ % SLAB _____ % CRAWL _____ % CONC. FLR.

HEATING: ☐ OIL ☐ GAS ☐ ELECTRIC ☐ RADIANT ☐ HOTWATER ☐ FIN & TUBE ☐ CAST IRON ☐ STEAM ☐ HOT AIR ☐ BASE ☐ CEILING ☐ FLOOR ☐ RADIATORS

AIR CONDITIONING: ☐ HUMIDIFIER ☐ CENTRAL ☐ SMALL UNITS

ELECTRIC: NO. OF SERVICES TOTAL AMPS ☐ BX ☐ PLASTIC ☐ KNOB & TUBE

PLUMBING:

	EXCEL.	GOOD	FAIR	POOR
WATER— ☐ COPPER ☐ BLACK IRON ☐ GALVANIZED ☐ BRASS				
WASTE— ☐ CAST IRON ☐ COPPER ☐ PLASTIC				

WATER: ☐ COMMUNITY ☐ DRILLED WELL ☐ DUG WELL ☐ SHARED WELL

SEWAGE: ☐ COMMUNITY ☐ SEPTIC TANK ☐ CESSPOOL ☐ WASHER DRY WELL

SIDING: ☐ CLAPBOARD ☐ WOOD SHAKES ☐ WOOD SHINGLES ☐ ASBESTOS ☐ STUCCO ☐ ALUM. ☐ ASPHALT ☐ PLYWOOD ☐ VERTICAL BOARDS

VENEER: _____ % ☐ STONE ☐ BRICK ☐ IMMITATION

STORMS: _____ % ALUM. _____ % THERMO _____ % WOOD ☐ ENAM. ALUM.

GUTTERS & LEADERS: ☐ ALUMINUM ☐ BAKED ENAM. ☐ GALVANIZED ☐ COPPER ☐ WOOD

LANDSCAPE: ☐ GRASS ☐ STONEWORK ☐ SHRUBS ☐ WALKS ☐ PATIO

DRIVE: ☐ ASPHALT ☐ DIRT ☐ GRAVEL ☐ CRUSHED STONE ☐ PEA STONE

GARAGE: ☐ CARPORT ☐ ATTACHED ☐ BASEMENT NO. CARS _____ ☐ DETACHED

COMMENTS:

ML971

4.
Borrow for Your Total Construction, Not on Your Unconverted Building Alone

When a bank appraiser inspects a building that a buyer wants to mortgage, he fills out an appraisal report like the one opposite. Along with questions shown here, he answers others about the neighborhood on the form's reverse side. (How is neighborhood zoned? What is the minimum lot size? Is this property typical?) He gives his report to bank officers, who decide whether to grant the loan.

Nine times out of ten, when the appraiser evaluates a building the buyer intends to live in, he reports on a conventional house with a heating system, electric wiring, and plumbing. But occasionally he finds himself looking at an old building and dealing with a buyer's dream. With no specifics to take to the bank, he can only report on what he sees.

Ask for a mortgage on a barn evaluated at $6000 and you will be lucky to get $3600. Submit a sound conversion plan for the same, and you can get ten times that or more.

Before talking to a banker, make an estimate as accurately as possible of what your conversion will cost. Ask your carpenter where to get the best buy on roofing, insulation, and plumbing. And then, *double check*! Also, get your carpenter's help on ways to use standard-size windows, weathered siding for inside trim, and old floorboards. Take your plan to a plumbing contractor for an estimate and to an electrician and to a heating contractor (or plumber) who will install your heating system. Get price from an excavating contractor (or anyone with a bulldozer) to dam stream.

Figure in the cost of a garage (perhaps with a guest apartment) that you want for later. During inflation, when labor, materials, and interest rates go up, borrow and build now rather than wait.

When you know how much cash you will need to convert, look with an appraiser's eye at your building *as it will be*. Will this home, when finished, be worth 30 percent more than what you will ask for at the bank?

Take your plans to a bank officer. (For the barn conversion, go with your floor plan for a home with two baths, three bedrooms, living room, dining room and den; plot plan; proposed materials. Ask about a mortgage commitment, but *don't apply for a loan until you know how much you will pay for your money*. At this stopping place you can save. Think of cash as a building material; shop for the best possible buy.

If you have a good credit rating, a bank wants your business as much as you want cash. So don't rush. If you can get money from one bank, you can get it from another.

Every bank you talk to will be looking for character, cash, income and property in your loan application. So do some assessing again. If you pay all bills promptly, as promised, you have a good credit rating and can be expected to *want* to pay. If you have cash (or a cash equivalency) you will be able to keep up payments on your mortgage even if you lose a job or find yourself in a squeeze for some other reason. If you have a good income, your banker can see how you can pay your mortgage and other expenses, too; and if your home obviously is going to be one that the bank can find a market for in case you default, you are a good risk.

Construction Mortgage Loan Payment Schedule

Amount of Loan $_____ Date_____ Mortgage #_____

I   <u>A Waiver of Priority of Mechanics Lien</u>: This will be furnished to you at the closing. You must have it signed by all persons and firms who have done work or have delivered materials to your premises. It must be signed by each owner and sworn to before a Notary Public. This waiver must be presented to the bank before any advances will be made.

II   <u>Insurance</u>: Evidence of fire insurance for at least the full amount of the mortgage must be presented at the closing. Policy must contain a mortgagee clause naming the New Milford Savings Bank as first mortgagee.

III   <u>Plot Plan</u>: The mortgagor shall provide a plot plan suitable for filing with the Town Clerk showing the location of the house, well and septic tank system with a certification by a registered surveyor that the lot and the buildings to be erected thereon conform to the planning and zoning regulations.

<u>1st advance</u> of $_____ will be made when the following have been completed.
1. Foundations completed.
2. House framed and entirely sheathed.
3. Roof completely shingled.
4. Rough flooring laid.
5. Carrying partitions in place.
6. Water supply in (drilled, dug or community).
7. Septic system in.
8. Plot Plan presented (see III above).
9. Written acceptance of septic system and well by sanitation official of Town.

<u>2nd advance</u> of $_____ will be made when the following have been completed.
1. Outside of house clapboarded or shingled.
2. Window frames and sashes in place.
3. Insulation.
4. Chimney and fireplace (except hearth).
5. Rough plumbing in place.
6. Heater set and risers in place.
7. Rough wiring installed.

<u>3rd advance</u> of $_____ will be made when the following have been completed.
1. Fireplace (hearth and mantel).
2. Floor covering (kitchen and bath).
3. Plumbing and plumbing fixtures.
4. Heating system in working condition.
5. Kitchen cabinets installed.
6. Driveway installed (hardtop - gravel).
7. Interior trimmed. Doors hung. Hardware set.
8. Flooring.
9. Tile work.
10. Interior walls.
11. Electric work.
12. All carpenter work.
13. Outside painting.
14. Inside painting.
15. Grading - seeding.

Approved: _____

_____

12/1/67

What you want from the bank is enough to convert your barn to a house as planned. In return, you are willing to pay interest on the money you borrow and to sign your home over to the bank in case you default. Fair, but take your time. (Pay ½ percent more interest than others are paying for a similar mortgage, and over a period of twenty years you will pay out in surplus interest enough to pay for a kitchen.) Go easy. And don't pay for "points."

When money is tight and buildings and buyers clamor for loans, many banks ask you to pay points in addition to interest just for the privilege of borrowing. Do not agree to a repayment penalty for paying in advance.

After talking to two or three banks, you will find one that understands what you want to do and will give you money at a satisfactory interest rate *(provided, of course, that your application is approved by the bank's officer)*. Remember when you apply that the more assets you have and the fewer liabilities, the happier the bank will be.

Once you get approval, read your contract carefully. *Caveat emptor!* (The caution "let the buyer beware" for buyers of real estate as a warning to examine property and assume conditions that are readily in view should be printed on mortgage contracts, too.) *Don't cheat yourself*. Ask for clarification if you don't understand, and insist on something better if a condition doesn't make sense.

If your application is accepted by the bank, you will receive notice to come to a closing, at which time you will be given the mortgage loan payment schedule.

As your workmen complete work, as spelled out in the form, your bank will send an inspector to see what has been done. On this inspector's approval, you will receive an advance on the loan against your home.

A closing is costly, so be sure that you ask for all the money you will need to borrow for your conversion when you apply for your loan. If you refinance, you will incur extra expenses including a new title search for a title searched only recently.

As work is completed on your home, you will be expected to notify your bank and pay for an inspection fee to get approval for what has been done. After each of the inspector's visits, you will increase your insurance, as agreed at the bank, to protect the lender who now has a sizable equity in the building. Usually, your fire insurance policy must contain a mortgagee clause naming the bank as first mortgagee.

You will save money as you build if you can be on the job with your carpenter, which he usually appreciates if this does not mean you are critical. You do not have to do actual carpentry along with your workmen, although your work cuts out the hourly rate for another carpenter, but your being around insures your carpenter's being supplied with materials. Then, he does not have to put down tools to restock. Also, you can advise him about what comes next so that he does not go off on a wrong track because he has not understood what you want.

If you work in a city and are building in the country, ask your carpenter to meet you at your conversion site on Friday night or Saturday morning to go over what he and his helper have done and will be doing in the coming week.

If you like to work with your hands, you can work on Saturday or Sunday or both, either in the building or outside. And if you're tactful, your carpenter, who is probably committed to go on to another job, will appreciate what you do. Probably your biggest problem will be a vague feeling of guilt that you should be doing more with your time than carpentry work. This vaguely apologetic feeling will pass as your home becomes more attractive because of your work.

Plan a beautiful remodeling job, and buyers will come if you ever decide to sell. Building a home is a joy in itself—and any profit will come automatically. Should you sell after years of good living, you may find that you have lived for free.

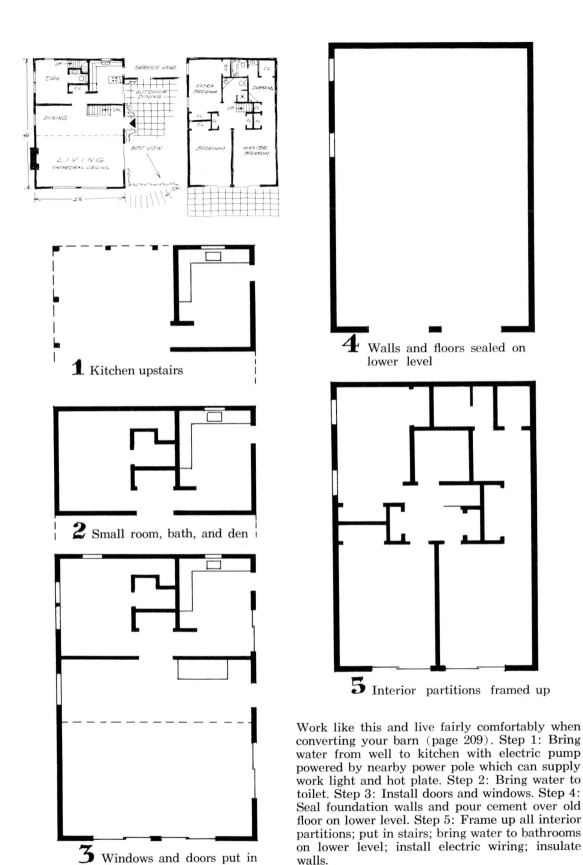

1 Kitchen upstairs

2 Small room, bath, and den

3 Windows and doors put in throughout

4 Walls and floors sealed on lower level

5 Interior partitions framed up

Work like this and live fairly comfortably when converting your barn (page 209). Step 1: Bring water from well to kitchen with electric pump powered by nearby power pole which can supply work light and hot plate. Step 2: Bring water to toilet. Step 3: Install doors and windows. Step 4: Seal foundation walls and pour cement over old floor on lower level. Step 5: Frame up all interior partitions; put in stairs; bring water to bathrooms on lower level; install electric wiring; insulate walls.

5.
Start with Basics, Keep Beauty in Mind

Working with the barn which we "bought" in Chapter 3 and "borrowed for" in Chapter 4 of this section, we will convert in a room-by-room sequence that makes sense for a family of four. We will suppose that you have hired a carpenter and his helper to work during week and you will "make do" on weekends.

Assuming that your roof is leakproof, you can stay in the barn immediately if you bring in water from the well and electricity from a nearby pole for a work light and a few electric appliances. If room is not in good condition, remove rotted wood shingles and put on new where roof can be patched, or cover entire roof with asphalt strip shingles (buying by the square [100 square feet] and figuring 10 percent should be added to roof area for waste). Let your children "camp out" in large upstairs barn area, and you stay in section that will be the den. Use chemical toilet until water comes to lavatory with toilet.

Now insulate and Sheetrock walls for den, kitchen, and lavatory, which will be back-to-back with kitchen. Bring water from the well for toilet, tub, and basin, and put hide-a-bed couch in the den for temporary sleeping and sitting quarters. Let the children use sleeping bags and play in 28 × 26-foot section that will be living and dining area.

Now, cut wall openings and install windows and glass doors, planning for privacy as well as outdoor-indoor look, ventilation as well as sunlight. For good ventilation, know the direction of prevailing breezes. Arrange for cross ventilation, and let the air enter at low point where warm air will rise and can

be exhausted at high point. Place clearstory windows high where privacy is called for in bathrooms and other areas.

For doors and windows, use insulated glass which gives as much protection as insulated wall.

Now seal foundation walls at lower level and pour new concrete floor over the barn's old base floor. Select insulation for walls that will work well with your heating system. (For system with conducted heat, put mineral wool or glass fiber between outer walls and Sheetrock to insulate barn. For radiant heat, use aluminum foil or aluminum coating, which reflects a high percentage of heat away from surfaces. Or combine fiberglass and aluminum insulation as your plumber or heating contractor recommends.) Carpenters can now frame walls for partitions for bedrooms and other rooms. Then, plumber can install tub, shower, and toilet in downstairs bath and bring in water through pipes that feed kitchen and bath above. Electrician can put in outlets, lights, and connections for heating units and kitchen equipment. Carpenters can build stairways and can panel or Sheetrock interior walls.

When "dirty work" is finished, you can lay tiles on floor at lower level and can sand, stain, and wax upstairs floor. If the floor is not in good shape, it can serve as the subfloor to be overlaid with boards or plywood to be stained or carpeted.

Converting this way, you have automatically built in beauty. Your large living room with its cathedral ceiling and huge glass windows in your proposed barn looks down on a sparkling stream. Below the patio, which will be flagstone or poured cement, is a swimming pond. The kitchen at back looks across a field and up into the woods. Here is where you will put your vegetable garden and fruit trees.

A big clean barn or similar "box" is a great buy, because you save by starting from scratch rather than trying to do away with the mistakes of another, which often happens when you remodel a house. But now you have to avoid mistakes.

One of the costliest is to botch up a kitchen, which many do. Yet the principles for good, practical kitchen design are easy to follow, as you will see below.

You bring food to your kitchen in bags which you put on a counter before putting your food into cupboards and refrigerator. Later, you will take this food out of both of these storage places and work at a counter where you will need water (so your sink must be beside counter). Then, you will cook your food on a range, which ideally should be near.

For obvious reasons, the "triangle" arrangement of refrigerator, sink, and range (top plan below) makes sense. In an expan-

sive kitchen, where there is much traffic and casual eating by many family members, the plan at bottom works well.

Her kitchen and bath are a woman's most important maintenance concerns, say many. She would like a guest apartment with a pullman kitchen, and has to have a guest bath. But the first is not always possible, and the second doubles as a family bath when guests are not there. So good planning for the entire house is essential.

Naturally, you save when you have a kitchen and bath, or baths fed by the same plumbing lines. But also consider size. You must have at least a 5 × 7-foot space to accommodate standard-size fixtures. If you want many bathrooms in a home and still want large rooms elsewhere, allot minimum space (as shown top plans below), then dress rooms up with novelty wallpaper, tile floor, a skylight, chandelier, or unusual window treatment or hanging plants. With more space, make less standardized use of space.

If you have a large family, consider a bathroom that lends itself to multi-usage. In last plan below, the toilet is enclosed in a small closet away from the tub and lavatory, and the dressing table is separate.

Two kitchen plans

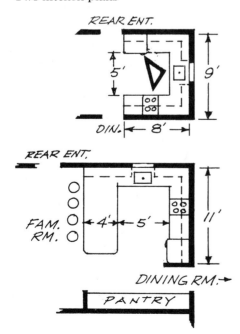

Four bathroom plans

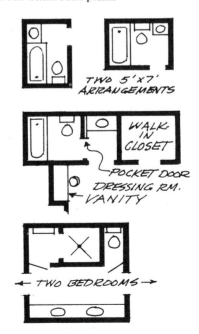

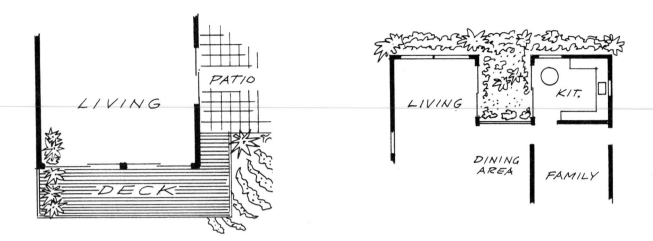

To insure privacy when buying a place to do over, buy as much land as your budget permits. Also, ask yourself, "How is the drainage? Where have neighbors hit water for a well? Do neighbors have a life-style unlike mine? Is a development coming? A gravel pit? Will there be noise from an airport? Is there a factory with a bad smell nearby? Will the stream overflow?" If there are negatives, can you compensate?

Get a copy of the topographical survey, made by the U.S. Geodetic Survey, of your land by calling the director of your county's Soil Conservation office who will tell you where and how much to send to buy. The map is inexpensive, makes a great wall decoration, and will help you as you plant and as you plan your driveway to drain properly.

Both landscape architects and remodeling experts urge you to plan your home and site as one, especially when your outdoor area is limited. Plan carefully to screen out undesirable sights, and extend the feeling of space.

On this page four drawings suggest ways to give a feeling of spaciousness to your home by extending the indoors out. In left above, living room, kitchen and dining area look out through glass walls to a garden with a glass roof which can be enclosed with glass panels as a greenhouse in winter.

Below left is a walled garden outside of a bedroom and bath with sliding glass doors. Wall is screen, rooms seem large.

Living room at top of column has floor-level deck outside of sliding glass doors, with no draperies, which open for indoor-outdoor living. Extended floor space opens up home for parties; provides play place for children separate from adults when doors are closed. Note how indoor plantings match those outdoors for room-extending impression.

Dramatic stone wall containing fireplace below carries eye outdoors to where same wall is side screen for deck. This see-through room with long view subordinates itself to outdoors.

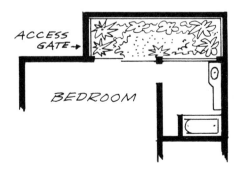

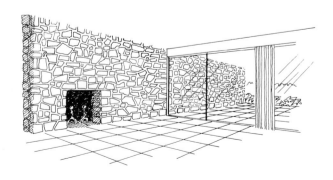

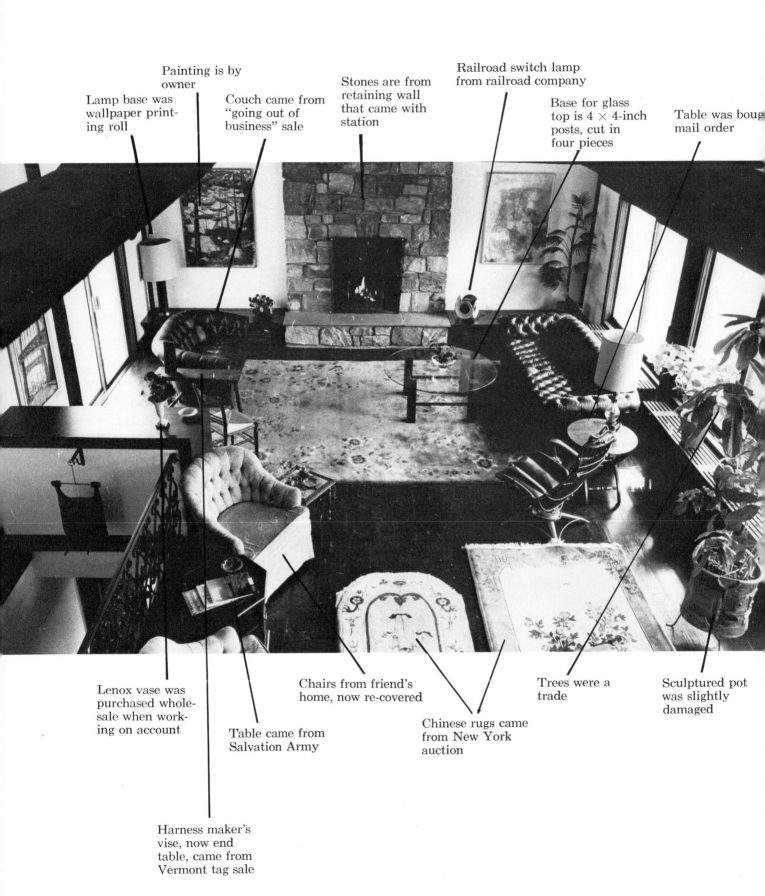

Lamp base was wallpaper printing roll

Painting is by owner

Couch came from "going out of business" sale

Stones are from retaining wall that came with station

Railroad switch lamp from railroad company

Base for glass top is 4 × 4-inch posts, cut in four pieces

Table was bough mail order

Lenox vase was purchased wholesale when working on account

Table came from Salvation Army

Chairs from friend's home, now re-covered

Chinese rugs came from New York auction

Trees were a trade

Sculptured pot was slightly damaged

Harness maker's vise, now end table, came from Vermont tag sale

6.
Ten Ways to Cut Back
When You Furnish Your Home

Artists often pay less for furnishings than owners of less attractive places pay for inferior things. Their taste is assured, so they dare to buy what others pass up; and they know how to buy for less.

Here are three rules they follow: (a) buy for your own taste only, not what the Joneses are buying; (b) buy item by item rather than in one fell swoop; (c) know the *why* behind every price that you pay.

Here are ten ways to get furnishings for less and why:

1. Buy from seller not in furniture business.

   WHY: Company wants to unload merchandise, rather than ship or invoice.

   EXAMPLE: We brought three railroad benches for $75 from Penn Central when nearby station closed. Our buy saved shipping bother.

2. Buy when working as volunteer at church or charity sale.

   WHY: All items are donated; any sale means profit. Volunteers get first chance.

   EXAMPLE: Friend bought Apache basket donated by couple who didn't appreciate Grandma's western souvenir.

3. Find prize at "going out of business" sale

   WHY: In-and-out furniture stores buy leftover stock from manufacturers and bankrupt stores which may include few good pieces. All will be unloaded; find the good.

4. Get slightly flawed merchandise for less.

   WHY: Factories sell seconds rather than ship to customers who may return. Craftsmen do same. Railroad salvage companies sell merchandise damaged in shipment. Artists sell "first try" paintings.

5. Get great buys at auctions.

   WHY: Auctioneers buy contents of home, sell by piece, don't want leftovers.

   TIP: Note bids of dealers. Pay a few dollars more than their offer and get quality.

6. Buy mail order.

   WHY: Maker of one item (game table, wood carving, sand painting) is testing price by mail. First buyers come out.

7. Make a trade.

   WHY: Someone will trade a painting or a piece of furniture when he can make more of the same, has no need for the piece you may want, or appreciates what you have to offer. Suggest trade that makes sense.

8. Buy from Salvation Army.

   WHY: Merchandise is donated, workers are often in rehabilitation program, transaction is cash. Seller can afford to sell for less and does. You can pick up unusual pieces here.

9. Buy wholesale.

   WHY: Wholesaler gets the same price if he sells to you or to customer who resells, but he refrains from selling retail because his customer will object. So you can buy this way only if you do work for wholesaler (as we did when we bought Lenox vase opposite), have a relative in the business, or can trade something you can buy wholesale for something another can buy.

10. Do it yourself.

   No WHY is necessary here. If you can make table, benches, chairs, wall hangings or anything else, you are ahead financially and have the fun of making things.

   Cultivate your taste, sharpen your eye, and don't be afraid to discuss price, and you will save as you furnish your home.

ENJOY

Near wife's Silo Shop (page 48) Skitch Henderson has studio in milkshed with silo 2 as sound chamber for pipe organ he bought for $75 at firemen's auction.

Wallboards from Vermont tanner's shed have dent marks where tanner nailed skins. Bricks are antique; pool is outside door; life for Ruth and Skitch is good!

ACKNOWLEDGMENTS

Trapper's cabin, Squash Hollow, New Milford, Connecticut, Dale Hartford, page vi.

San Francisco Zephyr, AMTRAK, page viii.

Photographs of Peter Fink's barn, before and after exterior and interior, pages 27, 28, 29.

Photographs of Kelleher home, Elizabeth Menzies, page 30; lower right, 31; upper and lower left and upper right, page 32. Kelleher home, Martin D'Arcy, lower right, page 32, upper and lower, page 33; bedroom pictures, pages 34 and 35. Architectural design information, courtesy William Shellman from office of Charles Agle, page 34.

Photographs of Kinney barn, New Milford *Times*, exterior, page 36; Waterbury *Republican*, exterior, upper left, page 41; George Bettencourt for *Scope Magazine*, stairway, page 42; Dale Hartford, interior photograph, page 43.

Photographs of Kelly home, Peter Fink, page 45; center and lower left and right, page 46.

Photograph of Ruth Henderson, *The Magazine*, page 48.

Photographs of Starobin silo, construction, Dr. Joseph Starobin, page 50; *The New York Times*, exterior, living room and bedroom, pages 50, 51, 53; Berkshire *Eagle*, ceiling, page 51; Unadilla Silo Co., silo design, pages 50, 52, 53; Laminated Products, Inc., page 52, drawings, L. M. Sehres, *Skiing* (© Ziff-Davis Publishing Co., by permission), page 52.

Photographs of windmill, Southampton College, pages 54, 55, 56, 57.

Photograph of Alex Ettl chicken coop, Ettl Farm, Princeton, page 58.

Photograph of turkey house, before, Rose Crohn, page 61.

Photographs of Amana house, Cedar Rapids *Gazette*, page 64.

Photograph of manger, before, Ray Boultinghouse, page 65.

Photograph of Gary Merrill at Maine lighthouse, Guy Gannett Publishing Co., Library, page 68.

Photographs for Dr. John F. Pick lighthouse on Lake Superior, Randi Ryoti, pages 69, 70, 71.

Photographs of exterior of Savannah warehouse, Historic American Buildings Survey, pages 72, 73; interior photographs of warehouse, Photography Associates, page 73; design, Juan C. Bertotto, architect, page 73.

Photograph of Bolivar lighthouse, Galveston News Co., page 79.

Watercolor, Old Field Light, Cyril A. Lewis, A.W.S., page 79.

Photograph of Spanish Stables, New Orleans, Library of Congress, page 80.

Photograph of door to Grant Wood's Carriage House, George T. Henry, page 81.

Photograph of sunporch, Mrs. Thomas M. Terry, page 83.

Photographs of Stern home, *Times Picayune*, New Orleans, pages 84, 85.

"Before" photograph, Ojai Stable, Marie du Var, page 86.

"After" photograph, Ojai Stable, Peter Darby, page 86.

Photographs of Jacksonville stable, Peter Darby, page 87.

Photograph of hot-dog stand, Samuel Smith, Brookfield, Connecticut, page 88; "after" picture, Dale Hartford, page 88; interior photograph, Dale Hartford, page 89.

Photograph of cabin deck, George Bettencourt, page 91.

Photograph of interior of bus, *The New York Times*, page 91.

Photograph of General Store, Earlham Library, page 92.

Photograph of construction of home from store, Des Moines *Register*, page 94.

Photographs of elevator and bedroom. Courtesy of Mrs. Robert J. Lewis, page 95.

Photograph of Dr. Powell's office (Mammy's cabin), Georgia's Stone Mountain, page 96.

Photograph of interior of lodge, Dale Hartford, page 97; photographs of lodge's fireplace, kitchen, dining room, Dale Hartford, pages 100, 101.

Design of New Orleans Duplex, Myrlin McCullar, New Orleans, pages 102, 103.

Photograph "before" of garage, Ed Lindig, page 104.

1900 photograph of home in Atlanta, Georgia, courtesy, Robert Griggs, page 106; entry hall, Robert Griggs, page 106; Christmas photographs of Griggs home, William A. Barnes, pages 108, 109, 110.

"Before" pictures, courtesy, office of Congressman John Culver, page 115.

From Universalist Church, North Salem, New York, "before" picture, page 116; interior photograph of church, Mrs. E. T. Nelson, page 119.

Photograph of "before" scene at Fort Lowell, Arizona Historical Society Library, page 122.

Photographs of fireplace, bedroom, dining room, date, William Sears, pages 124, 125, 126, 127; photograph of living room, Manley Associates, Tucson, page 128.

Photograph of William Talbot, Peter Fink, page 131.

Photograph of Stone children, New Milford, courtesy of Anna Mitchell, page 141.

Commemorative plate, courtesy of Mrs. Frederick Rarig, Gardenville, Pennsylvania, page 142.

Photographs of jail at Perrysburg, Ohio, *Bend of the River*, Perrysburg, Ohio, pages 144, 145.

Photographs of converted gas station, Paul B. Entrekin, pages 146, 147, 148.

Photograph of gas station before conversion, H. C. Stoddard, page 147.

Photographs of Chicago "cave," Art Detrich, pages 149, 150, 151.

Photographs of converted fire station's bedroom and dining room, Morley Baer, page 156.

Photograph "Old Folks' Day, Reunion"—1907—New Boston, New Hampshire, Public Library, page 159.

Photograph of interior of old mill, New Boston, New Hampshire, H. Randall Parker, page 161.

Postcard picture, The Jewel Mill, Rowley, Massachusetts, page 163.

Photograph, The Grist Mill, courtesy, Lawrence R. Kling, page 164.

Photographs of railroad station before conversion, Bridgeport *Sunday Post,* photographer Schulze, page 168.

Photograph of spring, New Haven *Register*, Dee Burghardt, page 169.

Photograph of railroad crossing, George Bettencourt for *Scope*, page 170.

Photographs of moving of station, Dale Hartford, page 171.

Photographs of Sheffield, Connecticut, station, Martha B. Porter, Sharon, page 182.

Photograph of converted station, Numa, Iowa, Jasper Frogge, page 182.

Photograph of Eric Sloane, courtesy of Sloane, page 185.

"Before" picture, Smyrna barn, Mrs. Max Don Howell, page 190.

Photographs of conversion of Howell home, Steve Hogden, pages 190, 191. Editorial courtesies, Edith Hills Coogler, Atlanta *Journal.*

Photograph of porch of Heights Hotel before conversion, courtesy Rep. John Culver, page 201.

"Before" picture of alley between buildings in Gaylordsville, Aaron Seltzer, page 202.

Photograph of Skitch Henderson, Dale Hartford, page 220.

All photographs and drawings not credited here to another source were made by Cle Kinney.

INDEX

228